Abortion: A Dialogue

Abortion: A Dialogue

Selmer Bringsjord

Hackett Publishing, Inc.
Indianapolis/Cambridge

Copyright © 1997 by Hackett Publishing Company, Inc.

Printed in the United States of America

02   01   00   99   98   97   1   2   3   4   5   6

For further information, please address
  Hackett Publishing Company, Inc.
  P.O. Box 44937
  Indianapolis, Indiana 42644-0937

Cover design by John J. Pershing

Text design by Dan Kirklin

Library of Congress Cataloging-in-Publication Data

Bringsjord, Selmer.
    Abortion: a dialogue/Selmer Bringsjord.
        p.   cm.
    Includes bibliographical references.
    ISBN 0-87220-367-0 (cloth)   ISBN 0-87220-366-2 (pbk.)
    1. Abortion—Moral and ethical aspects.   2. Imaginary
conversations.   I. Title.
HQ767.15.B75   1997
179.7′6—DC21   97-22044
                                                    CIP

The paper used in this publication meets the minimum requirements of
American National Standard for Information Sciences—Permanence of
Paper for Printed Library Materials, ANSI Z39.48-1984.

                            ∞

Contents

To my mother,
whose home was as intellectually lively as Bert's eatery

Preface

This dialogue is not a comprehensive treatment of the abortion controversy. (Since you have by now held the book and gauged its size, this shouldn't come as news to you.) The arguments at its core, however, are designed to spin out threads sufficient to weave a complete tapestry. The characters in this dialogue do a lot of weaving (especially for one day!), but they stop well short of the finished product. My hope is that they give you enough of a lead to finish the process.

Perhaps you're thinking: Can the process every really *be* finished? Is there really a fact of the matter as to the moral status of abortion? At least two of the characters herein believe so. Why—I can hear either of them asking you—should we regard problems in the realm of ethics to be forever unsolvable, whereas mathematicians can serenely assume that problems that have resisted centuries of intense reflection will sooner or later yield? And what—I can hear another of them asking—about slavery? Wasn't *that* a controversy at least as heated, and at least as complicated, as abortion?

I'm indebted to all those who have through the years debated these issues with me. Thanks to Jim Fahey for many helpful comments. In particular, it was Jim who long ago heard my early (more technical) version of the argument from the coma case discussed in Chapter 4 and provided valuable feedback. Finally, I'm deeply grateful to an anonymous referee for remarkably insightful comments on earlier drafts.

The Setting

Bert's Coffeehouse is located in prime protest territory, within convenient walking distance of the Supreme Court in Washington, D.C. Bert does a brisk business—and, believe it or not, an *orderly* business, thanks to the fact that patrons must abide by three rules posted prominently at the entrance to his eatery:

1. ALL PLACARDS, PROPS, AND OTHER PARTISAN PARAPHERNALIA ARE TO BE CHECKED UPON ENTERING.
2. OWNERS OF RAISED VOICES (OR FISTS!) WILL BE IMMEDIATELY EJECTED.
3. HALF-FILLED TABLES ARE TO BE SHARED.

It is a crisp, clear spring day in the capital. Charles, a young lawyer, spent the morning walking with his group of protesters, brandishing the twisted wire of a coat hanger while a placard announcing ABORTION SAVES LIVES! covers both his chest and back. Lauren, a young pediatrician, spent her morning across the street from Charles's group, carrying a tiny casket, dressed front and back with the proclamation ABORTION IS MURDER!

Upon entering Bert's for lunch, Charles and Lauren collide. Though they both dutifully check their incendiary equipment, they decide on the spot not to sit at the same table. But Bert's is hopping, and sitting separately proves impossible. They find themselves face to face at a table they must share with a third person: Alex.

Chapter 1

The Challenge Accepted

Alex nods a greeting to Charles and then to Lauren. Charles and Lauren don't even exchange a glance. Alex smiles knowingly.

ALEX: I bet the two of you checked some rather different items at the front.

Silence.

ALEX: What's the issue? Abortion?

Charles takes a deep breath, one deciphered by Alex as an affirmative.

ALEX: I see. Well, I'm allowed to bring everything to my table.

Charles and Lauren exchange glances but say nothing, and begin to tend to their sandwiches with dispatch.

ALEX: Not even curious, huh? I carry logic, nothing else. No signs or posters or explosive props. I travel light. Unfortunately, when it comes to abortion, logic is dead. The two of you, I daresay, are proof of that.

LAUREN: Abortion is a matter of the *heart*.

ALEX: True enough. When it comes to abortion, logic has certainly died. Problem is, it's harder to settle the issue with rancor than with reason.

CHARLES: The issue will never be *settled*. The issue will be *won*.

ALEX: Really? Show me, then; win me over. Without breaking Bert's rules.

Charles frowns and shakes his head. Alex turns to Lauren and makes the same invitation to her by raising his eyebrows. She too frowns and returns to her turkey on rye.

ALEX: All right, so be it. I accept my own challenge. I propose to win the two of you over to *my* side.

CHARLES: Oh? And what side might that be?

ALEX: Agnosticism. I'm agnostic on the issue; in fact, I'm a *proselytizing* agnostic.[1] I think the most powerful antiabortion argument that can be articulated *is* powerful—but is also ultimately uncompelling. Hence I don't believe that abortion is to be forbidden, nor do I believe that it's to be condoned.

Agnosticism makes for tolerance and peace, my friends. If you don't know the answer, and you *know* that you don't know it, you're not likely to scream and shout. . . . Now of course, maybe one of you *does* have the answer. In that case, I'd be much obliged if you'd share it.

LAUREN: The answer starts with the fact that human life begins at conception. "For Thou didst form my inward parts; Thou didst weave me in my mother's womb."[2]

*Lauren removes a small Bible from her breast pocket. Alex smiles and nods; then he taps his forefinger on Lauren's placemat, where Bert's rules are written. The finger falls specifically on "*ALL PLACARDS, PROPS, AND OTHER PARTISAN PARAPHERNALIA ARE TO BE CHECKED UPON ENTERING.*"*

ALEX: Actually, tell you what. I'll let you appeal to the Scriptures—as long as you first substantiate them by reasoned argument.

---

1. The names of our trio are intended to serve as mnemonics: Charles for the pro-choice position, Lauren for the pro-life position, and Alex for *a*gnosticism.

2. Psalm 139:13.

Charles allows himself a bit of a gloating grin and nods. Lauren herself relaxes a bit. Does the hint of smile touch the corner of her mouth?

LAUREN: How much time do I have?

ALEX: Not enough—given that, if you're to make any headway, you must address the principal reason I'm agnostic about the existence of God: suffering. I assume you read the papers. War, famine, earthquakes, hurricanes . . . why does God allow people to be tortured every day?

Lauren slides the Bible back into her pocket.

LAUREN: Fine. But if we're going to do this, we have to start *somewhere*.

ALEX: Right. If you're—sorry, I should know your name by now. I'm Alex.

They all share names.

ALEX: Okay. Well, Lauren, if you're going to convince me that abortion is immoral, you're going to have to show me by starting from what I *already* believe.

CHARLES: Good luck! This is morality, not mathematics. Sure, we learned back in high school that all *sorts* of surprising geometric truths can be extracted by careful reasoning from Euclid's postulates, a small set of propositions everyone believes to be true.[3] But here, in this mess, what are our postulates?

Alex nods and takes a sip of his coffee, nods some more. Then:

ALEX: Lauren, do you think slavery is morally wrong?

LAUREN: Of course.

ALEX: And you, Charles?

CHARLES: Ditto, obviously.

ALEX: Then I know where we can get our postulates. But before we begin, anybody need a refill?

---

3. The truth of the matter, as we now know, is that at least one of Euclid's postulates isn't unexceptionable—but we'll let this issue pass.

Chapter 2

Consensus

The three are seated again. The lunch crowd is shrinking. Bert's is quieting down.

ALEX: All right. So we agree that slavery is morally reprehensible. Why, exactly?

Alex waits for a few seconds. The expressions of the other two reflect interest, but there is no response.

ALEX: Okay, let's focus the question by imagining a concrete case: Suppose Striker is a white plantation owner. His wealth, his opulent mansion, the luxurious lives he and his family lead—all these rest on the backs of enslaved blacks who labor fourteen hours a day picking his cotton. These slaves are bought and sold like cattle; their families are broken up and distributed by Striker for profit. At times, Striker resorts to whipping his slaves; if their wounds become infected, he is often inclined to let them die instead of paying for medical attention. Sometimes, in order to "improve business," Striker shoots a slave outright, in plain view of the poor person's family. One slave who has suffered nearly the gamut of Striker's brutality is John. Now, again, how is it that we three condemn Striker's treatment of John?

CHARLES: Well, Striker is *hurting* John; he's hurting him severely.

LAUREN: But the answer must surely be a bit deeper than that. Lots of perfectly permissible behaviors hurt people: drilling cavities, depriving disobedient children of treats they desire, beating an opponent in a sporting contest, etc.

CHARLES: What I mean is that in hurting John as he does, Striker treats John as no more than a *machine*. If Striker's wealth rested on the capability of cotton-picking combines purchased in an ethically permissible manner, and he decided to discard a malfunctioning combine instead of repairing it, who would condemn him?

ALEX: No one. Machines aren't conscious; machines don't have hopes and dreams and beliefs; machines can't talk and reason and write and draw; slaves, of course, can. Is that basically it?

Charles and Lauren nod in agreement.

ALEX: Well then, friends, though Charles earlier reminded us that we aren't doing math this afternoon, it's easy enough to put our shared condemnation of slavery in the form of a somewhat pedantic but traditional-style *proof*.

Alex pencils out the following on the plain white back of one of Bert's placemats.[1] He passes it to Lauren. She reads it, nods, and passes it to Charles, who reads it and nods as well.

The Proof That Slavery Is Morally Wrong

Theorem. Slavery is morally wrong.

Proof. If x is an innocent person, then killing (maiming, torturing, incarcerating, whipping, selling, etc.) x is morally wrong. John is an innocent person. Ergo, Striker's treatment of John is morally wrong. *QED*

ALEX: Since this proof can be carried through for every slave, and for every slaveowner, we clearly have a demonstration that the *institution* of slavery is morally wrong.

CHARLES: Look, *we* accept the "proof." And maybe that does reveal some important "postulates" the three of us share. But not

---

1. The note-filled placemats arising from this dialogue appear at the end of this volume.

everyone will accept the reasoning we three find so agreeable. Let me play devil's advocate for a minute; maybe Lauren will join me.

Charles looks at Lauren; she nods acceptance.

LAUREN: Okay. It seems to me that if we are to resist the proof, we have three options. One, we can claim that slaves, though persons, aren't innocent. Two, we can claim that slaves simply aren't persons. Three, we can claim that slavery prevents some catastrophe or produces some boon that justifies treating some people as . . . as subhumans.

CHARLES: All right; let's see. The first claim is surely a dead end. The adjective "innocent" in the proof is a term that presumably holds of a person when he or she has not taken an action that makes that person a fair target for violence. For example, a robber who enters a bank waving a shotgun may well be shot by a guard—but if so, the guard, all things being equal, has done nothing wrong. In this case, the robber is not innocent.

ALEX: And perhaps you will agree that a related case arises in time of war, when a soldier fighting on the front lines is plausibly regarded to have forfeited his innocence, and hence can be permissibly shot by the enemy.

CHARLES: Okay. And obviously John has done nothing analogous to the armed robber or soldier. Right?

LAUREN: Agreed. What about the second claim—that John, and indeed all slaves, aren't persons? Can we say, as *rational* devil's advocates, that John, because he is black, or because he is "property," is a nonperson?

CHARLES: Of course not.

LAUREN: Then we are left with the third route. And maybe here we can make a go of our mock attack. Let's look a bit closer at the principle used in Alex's proof, namely . . .

Lauren circles the following part of the proof on the placemat.

If x is an innocent person, then killing (maiming, torturing, incarcerating, whipping, selling, etc.) x is morally wrong.

LAUREN: Maybe this principle, though *seemingly* true, really isn't, because in some extraordinary cases it *is* permissible to treat persons the way Striker treats John.

CHARLES: What sorts of cases?

LAUREN: Well, suppose some terrorists have set the countdown on an atomic bomb somewhere underneath the streets of Manhattan. The FBI locates the bomb with two minutes remaining, only to discover that the terrorists have assembled a human "shield" around the bomb, out of innocent kidnapped people. Removing this shield without loss of life would require hours of painstaking lockpicking. Some will surely say that the FBI can destroy the human shield in order to save millions of people who would otherwise perish.

ALEX: Interesting case. But how is Striker analogous to the FBI? More generally, what in the pre-Lincoln South even had a *chance* of justifying Striker's nefarious behavior?

CHARLES: Well, no doubt Striker himself, and others whose sybaritic life-styles come at the expense of slaves, might claim that to abolish slavery is to destroy their society, and that, they may go on to say, is itself a catastrophe. Not a bad hypo.

Lauren and Alex squint at Charles.

CHARLES: Short for "hypothetical situation." Law-school lingo, I'm afraid.

LAUREN: Ah. Well, actually, this line of argument was the chief justification for slavery offered prior to the Civil War. Are either of you familiar with Senator John C. Calhoun?

Alex and Charles shake their heads No.

LAUREN: In numerous Senate speeches, he argued that to abolish slavery would be to "attack the slaveholding States," and that since such an attack is a bad thing, slavery should remain firmly in place!

CHARLES: I think we can agree that such reasoning is unsound. For if it is not, then we would also have to accept a Nazi justifying the Holocaust by saying, "Yes, killing the Jews is evil. But if we don't continue to do it, and do it in secret, the Third Reich will fall—and that is a catastrophe the avoidance of which makes continued genocide permissible."

LAUREN: All right, but then how about this? Striker could claim that there is extreme positive good arising from the exploitation of John and his brothers, and that this good makes slavery worth it.

CHARLES: No, we have the same basic problem. Consider Nazi Germany once again. Suppose Hitler argued that the genocide he initiated and oversaw was worthwhile because it brought Nazis great happiness. Is this a good argument? Of course not. Even if, hypothetically speaking, genocide resulted in happiness on a grand scale, so that people not only inside but outside the Nazi Party were happy as a result, the killing of another ethnic group would be heinously wrong. Agreed?

Lauren and Charles nod.

ALEX: Then let's sum up where we are. If you bear with me as I write, we can rework our proof so that it takes explicit account of the possibility of the sort of catastrophe confronted by the FBI in the terrorist case.

Alex proceeds to adapt the earlier proof to the following new version, written on the back of an increasingly crowded placemat.

The (Explicit) Proof That Slavery Is Wrong

Theorem. Slavery is morally wrong.

Proof. If x is an innocent person, then killing (maiming, torturing, incarcerating, whipping, selling, etc.) x is morally wrong—unless such treatment prevents an extraordinary catastrophe that is itself a horrible evil. John is an innocent person. Striker's treatment of John does not prevent an extraordinary catastrophe that is itself a horrible evil. Ergo, Striker's treatment of John is morally wrong. Since 'Striker' and 'John' are names used to stand for any master and slave, respectively, what we have inferred about them can be inferred about slaveowners and slaves in general, from which it follows that the *institution* of slavery is morally wrong. *QED*

Charles and Lauren both read the proof and nod in affirmation of it.

CHARLES: But have we not simply spent a lot of time proving a truism? Of *course* slavery is wrong. I didn't need our discussion to discover *that*.

ALEX: But remember why we discussed slavery in the first place? I set us looking for a foothold from which we could tackle the abortion issue. I think we've found it.

LAUREN: And keep in mind, Charles, that our proof was not that long ago completely rejected by many, if not most, Americans, including many who were the most learned in the land. This seems to me to immediately establish at least the *possibility* that likewise in the case of abortion there may exist a proof that abortion is morally wrong. We just need to find it.

CHARLES: Wait a minute; slow down. Proofs can certainly be given in mathematics, and maybe, just maybe, it is not too much of a stretch to call the reasoning we have affirmed a proof. But abortion is quite another story.

ALEX: Maybe, but a point of logic, if I may, Charles. I don't think you should start by *assuming* that what we found for slavery we can't find for abortion. If the three of us can't continue in this with thoroughly open minds, then let's not continue.

Charles takes a deep breath.

CHARLES: Fair enough.

ALEX: And forgive me, but another point. You keep mentioning mathematics, Charles. Many concepts at the heart of mathematics are as murky as those at the center of our discussion. The concept of 'morally wrong' may not be transparent, but then again neither is 'number' or 'point' or 'set' and so on for a host of other concepts. If you're skeptical, you can prove me wrong by simply delivering a formal definition of, say, the concept of number. But be forewarned: after centuries of effort, there is still no consensus among mathematicians as to what, at bottom, a number is.

Furthermore, certain propositions concerning morality are, it seems to me, as indubitable as counterparts from the realm of mathematics. For example, I'm quite certain that $2 + 2 = 4$, but

I'm equally certain that it's morally wrong for someone to torture an infant for a bit of mild pleasure.[2] Do either of you disagree?

LAUREN: Not me.

Lauren looks at Charles.

CHARLES: I confess I do not disagree either. I imagine that some *would* disagree, but I confess I personally cannot. I can't look you straight in the eyes here and tell you that it's not morally wrong to torture an infant for pleasure. But I have a hard time imagining that my concession will have implications for the abortion question.

ALEX: Time will tell. But perhaps a pastry first?

The other two nod and, for the first time, smile outright.

ALEX: All right then. Let's recharge, and then we'll let Lauren try to make her antiabortion case.

2. Alex gives some thought to saying that it's plausible to think that there is a class of ethical statements (composed of statements like the one just cited involving torture) each of which is more "secure" than any statement in classical mathematics—but he decides that this is too far afield. The rationale behind Alex's unstated view is that classical mathematics is ultimately derivable from a few relatively simple axioms of set theory—but some of these axioms are open to question, and it is known, courtesy of a proof given by Kurt Gödel, that these axioms can never be shown by classical mathematical means to be without contradiction. See H. D. Ebbinghaus, J. Flum, and W. Thomas, *Mathematical Logic* (New York: Springer-Verlag, 1984) for coverage of these matters.

Chapter 3

A Red Herring

ALEX: All right, Lauren. We're ready. We three now know what a compelling argument in the domain of ethics looks like. Give us, if you will, such an argument for your position that human life begins at conception, and that therefore abortion is morally wrong.

Lauren takes a smooth, unhurried sip of coffee.

LAUREN: In order to determine when human life begins, perhaps you two will agree that it suffices to answer the following two questions.

Lauren writes out the following two questions on the back of the place-mat in front of her and passes them to her interlocutors, who nod to say Fair enough.

- How can you tell when something is human?
- How can you tell when something is alive?

LAUREN: Doctors harness science in order to heal; science is something I know a thing or two about. And science isn't silent on these two questions. The first can be answered immediately. What makes something human, rather than, say, canine, is the genetic material in question, and that material is readily observed with routine aids such as microscopes. I trust that both of you will agree that even a conceptus,[1] upon such examination, will reveal genetic material sufficient to classify it as a member of *Homo sapiens* rather than—excuse me—an embryonic Lassie.

CHARLES: And as to the question of determining when something is alive?

LAUREN: Easy, really. Scientists have produced a list of properties agreed, by consensus, to characterize life.[2]

Lauren pencils out the following list on the back of her placemat:

1. Life a pattern, not a specific material object.

2. Self-reproduction.

3. Storage of self-representation.

4. Metabolism.

5. Interactions with the environment.

6. Interdependence of parts.

7. Stability.

8. Ability to evolve.

LAUREN: Just in case this list isn't clear, bear with me as I explain it a bit.

Lauren taps each property on the list with her pencil as she proceeds.

LAUREN: Property number one. Life is a pattern in space-time rather than a specific material object. For example, most of our

1. The fetus at conception.

2. The following list is taken from J. D. Farmer and A. Belin (1992) "Artificial Life: The Coming Evolution," in C. G. Langton et al., pp. 815–40, and E. H. Spafford (1992) "Computer Viruses: A Form of Artificial Life?" in C. G. Langton et al., pp. 727–45—but this list can be obtained from countless other places in the part of the scientific literature devoted to specifying the attributes that distinguish living things. Sometimes the list is modified slightly, but such modifications leave the arguments of the present chapter intact.

cells are replaced many times during our lifetimes. It is the pattern and set of relationships that are important, not the specific atoms.

Property number two. A living thing must have the capacity to self-reproduce, if not in the organism itself, at least in some related organisms.

Number three. A living thing must store a self-representation. For example, contemporary natural organisms store a description of themselves in DNA molecules, which is interpreted in the context of the protein/RNA machinery.

Lauren taps item number four with her pencil.

LAUREN: The fourth property is having a metabolism that converts matter and energy from the environment into the pattern and activities of the organism.

Five. A living organism can respond to or anticipate changes in its environment. Organisms create and control their own local (internal) environments.

The sixth property of living things is interdependence of parts. The components of living systems depend on one another to preserve the identity of the organism. One manifestation of this is the ability to die. If we break a rock in two, we are left with two smaller rocks; if we break an organism in two, we almost certainly kill it.

Number seven. Stability under perturbations and insensitivity to small changes, which allow the organism to preserve its form and continue to function in a noisy environment.

Finally, property eight. The ability to evolve. This is not a property of an individual organism but rather of its lineage.

Sorry about the soliloquy. Any questions?

CHARLES: Continue.

LAUREN: Well, it's really quite simple. By this list, amoebae rightly qualify as living things. But the list is also satisfied by a conceptus, and all the more by a fetus later in the typical nine-month gestation period. So, it follows that the conceptus is both human and alive. So when does human life begin? At conception. QED.

Charles squints and takes a deep breath, his wheels spinning.

ALEX: Hmm. But where from here? Do you now have enough ammunition, Lauren, to show that abortion is morally wrong?

Lauren reaches for her mug and takes a sip. Then, in speech a bit slower than before, she continues:

LAUREN: Well, don't we know that taking human life is wrong? And haven't we just established that the fetus is human life?

ALEX: You don't seem too sure of yourself. A little parable may show that you're right to be tentative.

Imagine, Lauren, that you are an adventurous anthropologist who comes upon a tribe living in a hitherto-unexplored portion of a vast rain forest. And suppose that this tribe is divided into two classes, the masters and the slaves. Imagine, as well, that the treatment of slaves by masters in this tribe is as horrible, as sadistic, as violent as the worst behavior of Striker, the slavemaster we condemned in our earlier discussion. Now let's assume, furthermore, that though members of this tribe have an outward appearance that matches yours, the fact of the matter is that they have a genetic code that is *not* that of *Homo sapiens*. Though members of this tribe clearly communicate in a language, experience weal and woe, plan, dream, and in fact possess all the *mental* properties had by you and other humans, their DNA is not human DNA.

Charles begins nodding.

ALEX: Such a situation is entirely possible; it may be *unlikely*, but it's possible, and it drives home the point nicely: the evil slavemasters in this tribe are just that: evil. The fact that their genetic code differs from ours is not exculpatory in the least. Torturing some members of their tribe is just plain wrong, as wrong in the rain forest as in contemporary Western society.

LAUREN: Okay, I get it. Isn't the same point repeatedly made in popular works of science fiction, where alien races having a sufficiently rich mental life are presumed to have a right to life even if their physical bodies are somewhat different than ours?

CHARLES: Yes. For example, the popular show *Star Trek* and its follow-up, *Star Trek: The Next Generation,* feature many episodes in which nonhuman beings are justifiably accorded a right to life.

ALEX: Precisely. In fact, the possibility of alien life provides a way of putting a revealing question to our anthropologist: Suppose that humankind comes upon creatures who have all the psychological properties we have—these beings love and fear, debate and write poetry and create art, dream and hope, fall passionately in love, care for their offspring, and so on. But suppose that these creatures happen not to have the same genetic code humans do. Would it be okay to slaughter them?

CHARLES: Obviously, our hypothetical anthropologist would want to answer with a resounding No. But how could she if the principle behind her negative answer here is the one behind your condemnation of abortion, Lauren—namely, that killing something that bears the genetic code of *Homo sapiens* is wrong.

LAUREN: Look, I concede the point, Charles. In fact, now that I think about it, the argument that abortion is wrong because it involves the destruction of something that is both living and human is absurd. A living human cancer cell, for example, would be protected under this argument. But I assume we three agree not only about the immorality of slavery but also about the permissibility of chemotherapy.[3]

ALEX: What principle, then, *should be* the basis for Lauren's abhorrence of abortion, if she is to have any chance of providing a cogent rationale for her attitude? This question can be answered by divining what is at the heart of the desire, which we all share, to stop the evil slavemasters in the hypothetical rain-forest tribe. Here our previous discussions come to our aid. We agreed, perhaps even *proved,* that slavery, slavery of a sort seen in our own country's pre–Civil War era, is reprehensible. Now, what was at the heart of our desire to stop the evil Striker from brutalizing and killing his slave John? As we have now observed, the heart of our revulsion was *not* that John had some particular genetic code; rather, the key was that John and his shackled brothers possess properties at the heart of being a *person.* And what was the operative principle in our proof that slavery is wrong? As you may recall, it was this following one.

Alex circles the relevant sentence on the placemat:

If *x* is an innocent person, then killing (maiming, torturing, incarcerating, whipping, selling, etc.) *x* is morally wrong—

3. This point has been made by Don Marquis, "Why Abortion Is Immoral," *Journal of Philosophy* (1989) **89**: 185–202.

unless such treatment prevents an extraordinary catastrophe that is itself a horrible evil.

ALEX: Lauren's challenge, then, seems clear: it is to divine what a person is. Tied to the cases we have been pondering, her challenge is to discover those specific properties John has which give him a right to life and liberty. Any suggestions?

Alex picks up a pencil and is poised to record.

CHARLES: Okay. I would say that a person must be conscious. A person can experience pain and sorrow and happiness and a thousand other emotions—love, passion, gratitude, and so on—all properties that a fetus clearly does not—

ALEX: Let's develop the list a bit before we see where it leads on the issue, okay?

Charles registers agreement with a nod.

LAUREN: I would say that a person also communicates through a language, and knows and believes things, in fact has beliefs about what others believe.[4] A person also has desires. Desires not only for particular objects and events but also for more abstract things, like changes in one's own character.

ALEX: Pretty good. I'd add but two things. Persons are not only conscious but also are *self*-conscious: they are aware of their own states of mind, their inclinations, preferences, etc. A person, if you will, has a concept of self. Second, a person has what might be called a "will": a person makes choices and decisions and sets plans and projects—autonomously.

---

4. Lauren would appear to be on to something here. Lower animals perhaps believe and know as well, but a person can have what philosophers call *second-* and *third-order* beliefs. For example, persons can have beliefs about the beliefs of others (second order). A person, it would seem, can even have beliefs about what others believe about what they believe (third order). For instance, I believe that you believe, having reached this point in the book, that I believe personhood to be a key concept in the abortion debate. For a seminal discussion of these issues, and others relevant to our list (esp. property 5), see Daniel Dennett's "Conditions of Personhood," in A. O. Rorty, ed., *The Identities of Persons* (Berkeley, Cal.: University of California Press, 1976), pp. 175–96.

Lauren nods. Charles nods too but chuckles.

LAUREN: What?

CHARLES (to Lauren): We seem to be forgetting perhaps the one trait that has taken us from mutual contempt to calm coffeehouse conversation: Persons can *reason,* no?

Lauren, looking at Charles, nods a True enough.

ALEX: Okay, then here's what we have.

Alex passes around the list he has recorded. The others look at it briefly and affirm it without words. Here is the list:

A person

1. is conscious;

2. communicates through a language;

3. knows and believes things;

4. desires things;

5. is *self*-conscious;

6. has a "will"; and

7. reasons.

ALEX: Okay, not bad. Our list works smoothly to explain the verdicts we already arrived at: that the "masters" in the rain-forest tribe are wrong to enslave members of their society and that certain nonhuman creatures in film, TV, and novels ought to be granted a right to life. Additional confirmation of our list comes from a somewhat unlikely quarter: artificial intelligence. This scientific and engineering field—usually referred to simply as AI—though devoted to building artificial intelligences (robots, expert systems, etc.), rarely bothers to try to replicate, in the attempt to do so, *human* physiology. Instead, scientists and engineers in AI usually focus on trying to replicate the properties on our list in artifacts which, physically speaking, are nothing like us. Their assumption is that the psychological properties listed here, as opposed to having, say, eyes and ears like ours, are the essence of what it means to be a person.[5]

Nonetheless, as we shall soon see, our list is in need of modification—modification that yields an improved list that may well allow Lauren to prove that abortion, like slavery, is morally wrong.

Charles's expression says, This I've got to hear. But he gestures at the empty cups of the other two discussants. They both accept his offer of a refill with a grateful nod.

5. For an engaging, brief, nontechnical introduction to AI, see R. Wright, J. Dibbell, and G. Kasparov (1996) "Can Machines Think?" *Time* **147.13:** 50–58. For a technical introduction that will forge connections between personhood as it is used in this dialogue and (the notion of "agents" built in) AI, see S. Russell and P. Norvig, *Artificial Intelligence: A Modern Approach* (Englewood Cliffs, N.J.: Prentice-Hall, 1995).

Chapter 4

Lauren's Best Shot

CHARLES: Now Alex, I must confess that your last remark leaves me puzzled. You intimated that Lauren may have at hand a victorious antiabortion argument. But how can that be? You have led us in an investigation that has produced a list of properties that at least begin to capture personhood. But a fetus doesn't *have* these properties!

Charles slides the list back in front of Alex:

A person

1. is conscious;

2. communicates through a language;

3. knows and believes things;

4. desires things;

5. is *self*-conscious;

6. has a "will"; and

7. reasons.

CHARLES: With that list in front you, consider a one-month-old fetus. It is certainly undeniable that such a creature does not communicate through a language. It is also undeniable that such a being does not reason—because in order to reason as the three of us have today (in fact, in order to reason *at all*), it is necessary to have, among other things, a brain whose synaptic connections are at least mostly established, and that is something the one-month fetus, as our pediatrician can doubtless confirm, by definition lacks. As to the other properties on our list, it is certainly far from clear that they work out in Lauren's favor. It seems at least unlikely, for example, that a one-month-old fetus makes choices and decisions and sets plans and projects, and it seems just as unlikely that a fetus desires that its character be different. So why should Lauren's chances look good?

ALEX: For now, let's worry not about Lauren's case but rather about our list—which is problematic. And the reason is that the tense used in it is the *present* tense, a typographically tiny but ethically enormous fact. In order to see the problem, you have only to consider a simple extension of our slave case from our earlier discussion. Recall that Striker was a ruthless slavemaster and that John was Striker's "property." Now imagine that Striker, after seeing our list of person-relevant properties, reasons against us as follows.

"John is worth more to me dead than alive. Alive, he may pollute the minds of my other slaves with his notions of freedom; dead, he will be silent, and so sedition among his brothers will wither away. Shooting John is thus the answer to my problem. But so that my shooting John is morally acceptable even in the face of your list, I will put a bullet in his brain when he is in sound, dreamless sleep at 2 a.m. In this way I dodge the issue of personhood completely. This is so because at 2 a.m. John is not a person by your own definition, for at this time he isn't communicating through any language. In fact, at 2 a.m. John simply isn't conscious; he's asleep!"

Are we agreed that this reasoning is flawed?

CHARLES: Yes.

LAUREN: Of course. To bring the point closer to home, the question How many people were asleep at 2 a.m. in your house last night? is certainly a perfectly meaningful one, and easy enough to answer. But if Striker's reasoning is valid, it follows that there were *no* persons asleep in your home last night at two. In fact, from

Striker's reasoning, it follows that there can be no such thing as a sleeping person!

The two men nod.

ALEX: And the solution is?

LAUREN: Well, perhaps it's worth observing that John, when asleep, certainly has the *capability* or *capacity* to communicate in a language; likewise, he retains, even while snoring, the *capacity* to reason and to desire and so on for the other properties on our list. Proof of this is easy to come by: one has only to wake John and then engage him in conversation.

ALEX: Sounds good. This makes fixing our list effortless.

Alex pencils in a few quick but potent changes to the list, yielding:

A person is a being having the *capacity* to

1. be conscious

2. communicate through a language;

3. know and believe things;

4. desire things;

5. be self-conscious;

6. "will"; and

7. reason.

CHARLES: When the reasoning we used to condemn slavery is conjoined with this amended list, the immediate and welcome consequence is that Striker's Machiavellian dodge is cut off. Striker is prohibited from killing the sleeping John, for even while asleep John counts as a bona-fide person, and hence has a right to life.

ALEX: Exactly. Now let's certify this result with a more careful version of the proof that slavery is morally wrong. In preparation for doing so, let's refer to our improved list as . . .

Alex writes the symbol L above the list in question.

ALEX: *L*. This symbol will allow us to refer to the list without having to repeatedly enumerate all its entries. Here's the more careful proof I have in mind.

Alex pulls the previous antislavery proof over in front of him and, with pencil, on another placemat, produces the following:

The Careful Proof That Slavery Is Wrong

Theorem. Slavery is morally wrong.

Proof. If *x* is innocent, and has the capacities enumerated in list *L*, then killing (maiming, torturing, incarcerating, whipping, selling, etc.) *x* is morally wrong—unless such treatment prevents an extraordinary catastrophe that is itself a horrible evil. John is innocent and (even while asleep) has the capacities listed in *L*. Striker's treatment of John (whipping, killing, . . . him) does not prevent an extraordinary catastrophe that is itself a horrible evil. Ergo, Striker's treatment of John is morally wrong. Since 'Striker' and 'John' are names picked at random, what we have inferred about them can be inferred about slaveowners and slaves in general, from which it follows that the *institution* of slavery is morally wrong. *QED*

ALEX: Do the three of us affirm this proof?

Lauren nods.

ALEX: Charles?

Charles nods now as well, but slowly. Does he see now where Alex is going?

ALEX: Okay. Now. There is a principle in our proof that is so important I think it may be worth isolating it. I call it the Silver Principle, and it runs as follows.

Alex writes out the following principle, looking back to the proof for reference as he does so.

The Silver Principle

If

- *x* is innocent, and

- *x* has the capacities enumerated in list *L* (which together say what it is to be a person),

then killing (etc.) *x* is morally wrong—unless such treatment prevents an extraordinary catastrophe that is itself a horrible evil.

Lauren inspects the principle. She nods and slides it over to Charles. He reads it, takes a deep breath, and ponders. Then:

CHARLES: But suppose, Alex, that Striker, our slavemaster, is fiendishly resourceful. He thinks he sees a way to take John's life without doing violence to our new and improved list, and the Silver Principle. Specifically, imagine this: John, after toiling for countless hours in searing heat, loses consciousness. Striker then reasons as follows.

"John is so sick that he no longer even has the *capacities* that, according to your list *L*, together make him a person. Not only is he not communicating at present, but he isn't *able* to communicate in his current state. The only way John is ever going to regain consciousness is if he is ministered to; whether or not he ever communicates or reasons or wills or dreams or laughs again hinges completely on what *others* do—on whether I bring a doctor in. John himself no longer has the capacity to do *anything*. Hence, John is no longer covered by the Silver Principle, and I can shoot him as I would shoot an animal who threatens the productivity of my plantation."

I submit that once again we must agree that there is something seriously wrong with Striker's reasoning. As we have unshakably confirmed, slavery *is* wrong; and since slavery is wrong, it surely must be wrong for Striker to shoot John dead both when he is well *and* when he is ill. But *why* is it wrong for Striker to destroy John? If the Silver Principle won't do the job, what will?

ALEX: Good case; good question. But before addressing your question, perhaps it's worthwhile to consider a scenario that falls a bit closer to home:

Your dear friend Amy, let us suppose, has been in a bad car accident. You arrive at the hospital to find that she is in a coma. The prognosis, you are relieved to hear, is good—but at the moment Amy's brain activity is depressed, so low, in fact, that she, like John, lacks the capacities on our list. Amy no longer—

LAUREN: Excuse me, Alex, but in order to be a bit more careful about Amy's state, we can refer to the Glasgow Coma Scale, which doctors use to rate the probability that the patient will return to normal functioning.

ALEX: Okay, good. Amy no longer has the capacity to communicate, love, reason, etc., but her score on this scale indicates that she will come back. Now, in this situation, would it be okay for the doctor in charge to give Amy a lethal injection and then proceed to distribute her organs? How would you react if this doctor serenely said, "Well, Amy no longer enjoys the capacity to reason or communicate or love and so on. This puts her outside the purview of the Silver Principle. Hence we can with impunity inject her and farm out her organs."

I think you would probably question this doctor's sanity (let alone his moral sensibility). But then, once again, the Silver Principle must certainly be missing something. What?

Charles takes a sip of coffee, leans back, and reflects.

LAUREN: Let's see. We need to ground a prohibition against Striker's (and the doctor's) failing to minister to the ailing but curable John (and Amy). But what is it in such situations that makes the actions we know to be wrong wrong? . . . Okay, I think I've got it. The reason why Striker ought to save the ailing John from dying in his bed, and the reason why the doctor ought bring back the comatose Amy is that *both John and Amy will, if appropriately treated, return to a state wherein they enjoy the properties on our list L.* In short, if they are cared for, they will both once again enjoy the full fruits of personhood.

Charles frowns but offers no objection.

ALEX: It seems, then, that we arrive at a slightly more sophisticated principle—something I propose to dub the *Golden* Principle. The basic idea behind this principle is short, sweet, and compelling. It is this: One must grant a right to life to those beings who are innocent and have, or *will have,* personhood. Put more precisely . . .

Alex goes to work on the placemat, adapting the Silver Principle. Presently he passes the following around.

The Golden Principle

If

- *x* is innocent, and

- *x* has, or *will* have—because of a chain of events that can be kicked off by a person *y*—the capacities enumerated in list *L* (which together constitute personhood),

then it is morally wrong for *y* to destroy, or to authorize others to destroy, *x*—unless such destruction prevents an extraordinary catastrophe that is itself a horrible evil.

ALEX: I know it looks complicated, but it's really not. The basic idea is quite straightforward.[1] The Golden Principle, encapsulated, says that those who have, or will have, the psychological powers distinctive of persons should be protected. Striker fails to protect John; our nefarious doctor fails to protect the comatose Amy. As to the "causal chains" in these two cases, they should be pretty obvious, at least in broad strokes. In the case of both John and Amy there is a set of actions (administering drugs, providing appropriate fluids, running diagnostic tests, and so on) that, working in conjunction with the laws of medicine and biology, will eventuate in their recoveries.[2]

1. There are, however, certain niceties that would ultimately need to be included. First, there should be an insertion made to the effect that the causal chain of events need only be a high *probability*, not a *certainty*. (In the coma case, you and the doctor can only know that, if appropriately treated, your friend Amy will *probably* regain full-blown personhood.) Second, the person *y* must certainly know of the causal chain in question, and must also know that he or she can enable it.

2. You may wonder whether the Golden Principle is unprecedented. I frankly do not know. I do know that Don Marquis, in his argument that abortion is nearly always immoral ("Why Abortion Is Immoral," *Journal of Philosophy* (1989) **89**: 185–202), appeals to the principle that it's morally wrong to take the life of an individual who will probably enjoy a future

LAUREN: I take it that the Golden Principle points a finger specifically at those who have it within their power to safeguard the personhood of the protected individual. In the case of Amy, it is the *doctor* who is expressly forbidden from taking her life—because it is the doctor who has it within his power to return Amy to a thriving state. Right? Likewise in the slave scenario, it is *Striker* who is condemned if John dies—because it is Striker who has it within his power to see to it that John survives. In this regard the Golden Principle, on my reading, is quite cautious, and possibly more limited than it needs to be.

ALEX: Perhaps you're right. After all, even if Striker's wife is a thousand miles from her plantation home and knows nothing of John's plight, it would seem correct to say that she is morally prohibited from taking John's life—but since she can't play the role of *y* in the principle, the Golden Principle cannot be what undergirds this prohibition.

Charles stares at the Golden Principle, lost in thought.

ALEX: Finally, note that the Golden Principle provides a plausible explanation for why in some cases euthanasia is permissible. If an individual ever reaches a point in time where he or she no longer has the capacities that constitute being a person, *and* it's true that this individual can never regain these capacities, then the Golden Principle doesn't apply. In other words, the Golden Principle is quite consistent with our intuitions that trauma victims who literally lose essential parts of their brains ought to be allowed to pass on, free of machines that keep their hearts and lungs operating.

Alex and Lauren notice that Charles is miles away.

ALEX: Charles? Charles?

CHARLES (without looking up): I see it.

---

like ours. What Marquis fails to notice, apparently, is that those things about our futures that have most value invariably fall at the heart of what makes us *persons*. In general, however, Marquis's position is similar to the antiabortion argument Alex is steering his interlocutors toward, and I'm thankful to Jim Fahey for directing me to Marquis's paper after hearing, a number of years back, the "person-based" case against abortion I'm now articulating through our trio.

Charles now looks up—directly at Lauren, and then Alex.

CHARLES: I see the argument. Correct me if I am wrong, Alex, but here is how I think it runs.

Suppose, again, that I have a friend, Amy, who is thrown into a coma as a result of a car accident. As a result, she does not have an inner life: she doesn't hope, reason, fear, judge, love, dream, plan, and so on. Moreover, she doesn't even have the *capacity* to do such things. Suppose that I am Amy's guardian; suppose also that Amy's score on the Glasgow Coma Scale is high enough for her to be considered "fully retrievable." Would it be permissible for me to allow someone to kill Amy? Obviously not. Now, a fetus with chances slimmer than Amy's is the exception rather than the rule; indeed, biology being what it is, we know that the fetus will before long have a mental life on par with ours, assuming it receives the standard and requisite care (which is care less extensive than that which Amy has a right to). Hence a fetus presses upon its parents and/or guardians and involved others (e.g., doctors) prohibitions as serious as those Amy-in-the-coma presses against me and those in a position to abort her recovery. Since I am prohibited from taking Amy's life, we are prohibited from taking the life of a fetus. Abortion is morally wrong.

Is that basically it?

ALEX: Lauren?

LAUREN: Yes, and let's make it as fancy as its predecessor.

Lauren takes the time to write the antiabortion argument out as the disproof of slavery was:

The Antiabortion Argument

Theorem. Abortion, except in certain exceedingly rare cases, is morally wrong.

Proof. First, we reiterate the Golden Principle:

If x

- is innocent, and

- has, or *will* have—by virtue of a causal chain of events that can be enabled by the actions of a person *y*—the capacities enumerated in list *L*, *then* it is morally wrong for *y* to destroy, or to authorize others to destroy, *x*—unless such destruction prevents an extraordinary catastrophe that is itself a horrible evil.

Next, consider some fetus *F,* and some parent *P.* Fetuses are innocent (since they have done nothing to threaten others—a fetus can't really *do* anything, after all); hence *F* is innocent. *P,* save for some *rare cases,* has it within his or her power to enable a causal chain of events leading to a point in time when the fetus *F* will have the capacities at the heart of personhood enumerated in list *L.* It follows immediately that it's morally wrong for *P* to destroy *F,* which is to say (since *F* and *P* are general variables standing for any fetus and parent) abortion is morally wrong. *QED*

Alex quickly scans Lauren's prose; then he slides it over to Charles, who reads it in earnest.

CHARLES: Not bad; not bad at all. I notice that you say, "save for some rare cases." Perhaps our first order of business at this point is to establish the exceptions that even *you* grant.

LAUREN: Sounds good.

CHARLES: All right, so what do you have in mind?

ALEX: Perhaps I can take a stab first . . .

With head down, eyes on the proof in question:

ALEX: The proof doesn't apply to parents who are unable to ensure that their children reach a point at which personhood blooms. In war-torn countries, for example, parents may simply be unable to see to it that their children progress. This may be the case because these parents are critically injured, or because their children are kidnapped, and so on. *P* here . . .

Alex taps this point in the proof.

ALEX: . . . must stand for a parent who *can* ensure that the fetus in question reaches a point in time when he or she has a capacity to love, reason, communicate, and so on.

Lauren nods.

LAUREN: Of course, the method an adult follows to ensure the growth of a fetus, infant, or child can include reliance upon others.

In fact, in some cases the only option open to parents intent on enabling their child to enjoy the blessings of personhood is to give this child into the care of others.

CHARLES: And other exceptions?

LAUREN: Well, I suppose the paradigmatic exception arises when the fetus simply cannot reach the capacities at the heart of person-hood. Consider, for example, an acephalous fetus, that is, a fetus without a head. Such a tragic birth defect obviously precludes the fetus from ever reaching *any* of the capacities involved.[3] Because of this, the Golden Principle is not activated—its "if" part is never true. I take it to be a virtue of the argument that it allows for the intuitively desired exception in this case.

Silence.

CHARLES: I need to think about this. And at this point, in order to think, I am going to need dinner. What about you two?

---

3. In this case, the fetus, morally speaking, may perhaps be reduced to the level of a mere animal. The Golden Principle does not prohibit the killing of animals—which may be an intuitively pleasing result, because most of us hold that killing animals (at least in some cases, e.g., in order to generate food) is often permissible.

Chapter 5

Charles Regroups

The three have eaten. Charles looks especially refreshed. He is making some notes for himself on his placemat. He finishes writing and looks up.

CHARLES: I believe I have regained my balance. Ready to resume?

Lauren nods. Alex answers in the affirmative by clearing the remaining dishes off their table. Bert himself is now back, apron tied around his waist; he smiles and nods knowingly as Alex brings the dishes to the counter. Bert isn't the least bit surprised to find that three of his patrons have been in his establishment for hours. Nor is he surprised that Alex, once again, is managing to heal a visceral clash with the balm of sweet reason. When Alex returns to his seat, Charles kicks things off without delay.

CHARLES: Okay; here goes. The antiabortion argument now on the table is, I concede, interesting. But in the end it doesn't work. I begin with a fact that you have forgotten to mention, Lauren: that it is permissible to kill persons, and potential persons, in *self-defense.*

Suppose that you wake one morning to find that you have been abducted during the night and are now hooked by some machinery to a man making use of your kidneys. This man's own kidneys have failed, no organs for transplant are available, and, desperate, his loved ones have seen to it that your kidneys will now be shared with him—for nine long months.[1] Clearly, you have a right

---

1. This resembles a famous thought-experiment devised by Judith

to defend yourself; it's morally permissible for you to escape, even if extricating yourself means that the man with the failing kidneys will die. Likewise, a pregnant woman can "extricate" herself from the fetus "hooked up" to her body. Abortion, you see, can be a form of self-defense, because the fetus, if brought to term, does great violence to a woman's life.

Alex nods and looks at Lauren.

LAUREN: We originally visited the issue of self-defense when we agreed that people can take certain provocative actions that make them fair game for violent treatment. The example we considered was that of an armed robber who enters a bank brandishing a shotgun. Such a person can be permissibly shot in self-defense by security guards.[2] The robber, in such a scenario, is not—in our sense of the word—*innocent*.

Now, if memory serves . . .

Lauren looks for the right set of notes on one of their placemats.

LAUREN: Ah. We explicitly considered the innocence of the fetus in the proof Alex helped us construct. And we *had* to: for the Golden Principle, as you'll recall, protects only innocent individuals.

Lauren slides the appropriate placemat in front of Charles, with her fingertip suitably placed upon it.

LAUREN: I claimed that a fetus is innocent. This claim was made on the strength of the following rationale, which I left unspoken. If an individual is no longer innocent, in the sense that it can now be justifiably killed, then this loss of innocence must come by virtue of some action taken by that individual. In the case of the robber, the action is entering a bank armed with a shotgun.

Jarvis Thomson in her well-known defense of abortion: "A Defense of Abortion," *Philosophy and Public Affairs* (1971) **1.1**: 47–66.

2. While some might be inclined to say that the guards here ought to pursue other, less violent options, that might not be possible. Imagine that the robber, immediately upon entering the bank, shoots one bystander dead and then presses the barrel of his shotgun against the forehead of a guard, with his finger tightening around the trigger. Surely in *this* case the guard can shoot the robber in self-defense.

But what has the fetus *done* to void its right to life? What has it done to forfeit its innocence? Nothing—because a fetus isn't capable yet of doing *anything*. I readily grant, of course, that bringing a fetus to term can be—no, *invariably is*—a very difficult thing. But it hardly follows from this that the fetus can be killed in self-defense. Imagine, for confirmation of this point, that Striker, our representative slaveowner from earlier conversation, reasons as follows:

"In your purported proof that slavery is morally wrong, you have neglected to note that it is permissible to kill persons, and potential persons, in *self-defense*. Suppose that you wake one morning to find that overnight your house and business have been reduced to mere rubble, because your employees, your slaves, have been unshackled. Clearly, you have a right to defend yourself and your family from ruin; you have a right to keep property you lawfully purchased. Forcing your slaves to stay, you see, can be a form of self-defense, because abolition, my friend, spells doom for a cotton plantation."

Do you find this reasoning compelling, Charles?

CHARLES: Of course not. But this isn't the reasoning behind my objection.

You have said that the fetus cannot perform any premeditated actions, and hence cannot be anything but innocent, and in turn cannot be harmed in self-defense. My objection is that there are cases wherein person *x* kills person (or potential person) *y* in self-defense even when *y* has performed no premeditated actions and is therefore thoroughly innocent. Consider, for example, the following case.

A terrorist group has acquired a powerful short-range missile system and has kidnapped a number of the opposition, citizens of a country the terrorists seek to destroy. The terrorists devise a gruesome plan: they strap some of the kidnapped innocents onto the missiles and then launch the missiles at the hated country. The threatened country possesses a missile-defense system, but if the system is deployed, it will not only destroy the incoming missiles but also of course the innocent citizens strapped to them. If the missiles reach their intended targets, urban centers, the carnage will be incalculable. What should the country do?

Though the question isn't directed at him, Alex answers:

ALEX: Though it will be an excruciating decision, it seems to me that the right thing for the threatened country to do (assuming evacuation is impossible), tragically, is to destroy the incoming missiles before they land. If this *isn't* done, millions of citizens, if I understand your case, would be vaporized.

CHARLES: Exactly. But then it follows that it is sometimes morally permissible to kill innocent people in self-defense even when they have not performed any relevant actions.[3]

LAUREN: But how helpful can this analogy be? After all, these poor people will die no matter *what* is done. Doesn't this make the case a morally easy one?

CHARLES: Hmm, true. So let's consider a slightly different case. Some terrorists instruct our government to kill a certain innocent person. Failure to do so, they say, will "force" them to trigger some catastrophe, say a nuclear explosion. Suppose, specifically, that the innocent person would *not* die in the explosion. Now here we have a case where . . .

LAUREN: No; Charles, you're running into a dead end. Even if I agree for the sake of argument that the government does nothing unethical in killing the designated innocent, you have a problem. Both in your new case and in the missile case, the fact is that the government is defending itself *against the terrorists*. How is this analogous to abortion? If an abortion isn't acting in self-defense against the fetus (just as your nations don't act in self-defense against the innocents), then who is being defended against when an abortion is performed?

Pause.

CHARLES: In the case of pregnancy due to rape, an abortion can constitute self-defense against the rapist, with the fetus caught in the middle.

---

3. Cases such as the terrorist one just given are related to the Catholic doctrine of "Just War," the distinctive feature of which is that actions whose unintended side effects result in the death of innocents may nonetheless be permissible in time of war. World War II would presumably be a real-life case.

LAUREN: I can go along with that. But this just means that you have found another exception, another one of those "rare cases," which the antiabortion proof explicitly accepts.

Lauren's finger finds the "rare cases" phrase in the proof; she underlines it for Charles to see.

LAUREN: Another family of such cases would presumably include situations in which the fetus threatens the mother's life, as in an ectopic pregnancy.

ALEX: But the problem you face, Charles, is that such cases are, as the phrase says, *rare*. The question is What do you do with the vast majority of pregnancies? Add up all the ectopic pregnancies, all those involving severe birth defects, and then add pregnancies due to rape—add them all together and, in America, anyway, you have less than three percent of pregnancies. What about all the "normal" cases?

Charles nods as he reflects.

ALEX: Your kidney thought-experiment seems disconnected from the mainstream cases. It seems to apply only to the rape situation; for therein, like the victimized mother in the case of pregnancy due to rape, you did nothing to bring it about that you were kidnapped and hooked up to the desperate man. But in the preponderance of pregnancies, this is not the case. Pregnancy usually results from voluntary sexual intercourse, and it's rather well known that such activity often leads to pregnancy. If you had done something to cause the desperate man to lose the use of his kidneys, then you would doubtless have less latitude in how to respond permissibly upon waking to find tubes running out of your abdomen.

Charles sips some of Bert's aromatic Blue Mountain brew, glances at his notes, and ponders. Then:

CHARLES: Look, suppose I know that there is a chance that if I bed down for the night in anything less impregnable than a bank vault, I may wake to the horror of finding myself strapped to the man whose kidneys are failing. (To make this plausible we can suppose that there have been reports of similar nocturnal abductions in the area.) If I nonetheless go to sleep and, alas, wake to find myself hooked up, it is undeniable that I have done something that causally contributed to the man's being hooked to me: namely, I went to bed! And yet in this situation, despite the fact that my actions have contributed to my plight, and to the man's dependency on me, I don't think we'd want to say that I must allow the man the symbiotic use of my body. Similarly, the mere fact that a man or woman may have done something that he or she knows makes it possible for pregnancy to occur doesn't immediately imply that she cannot "unhook" herself from the fetus.

LAUREN: I must say, Charles, you seem to have a penchant for stretching the bounds of analogy. Fetuses don't demand anything like what the kidney-needing man demands! I've carried three; I've cared for countless. A pregnant woman isn't usually strapped down to a bed.

CHARLES: But even normal pregnancies, as you must well know, are disruptive, no?

Lauren's expression is noncommittal.

CHARLES: All right, look, let me change the case a bit.[4] Suppose, Lauren, that you are kidnapped by a mad scientist who plans to hypnotize you to have a permanent mental block against all your medical knowledge. Such hypnosis would destroy your career in pediatrics, which would in turn have a serious adverse impact on your family, your personal relationships, and your happiness. By my lights, if the only way you can avoid this outcome is to kill the attacker when he comes, you are morally justified in doing so. And it does not seem to be an exaggeration to claim, as I do, that unwanted pregnancies often have consequences as bad as your loss of livelihood.

LAUREN: No, I still don't buy it. Bringing a baby to term almost invariably doesn't entail a loss of livelihood, at least not in the long term. But at any rate, you have *another* problem. We all need to sleep; if we don't sleep, we don't live. Voluntary sexual intercourse is different: it's just that: *voluntary.*

CHARLES: True. But *driving* is voluntary. Yet we don't blame you for your injury, or those of your passengers, if a traffic accident

---

4. The following case is adapted from Jane English's "Wrongs and Rights," *The Canadian Journal of Philosophy* (1975) **5.2:** 233–43.

befalls you. Why should sexual activity be any different? Yes, such activity is voluntary; but if pregnancy befalls the female participant, why should we hold her to standards higher than those we use to judge motorists?

LAUREN: Motorists aren't *always* off the hook. If you drink and drive, and have an accident, we blame you. If you drive in a blizzard when you don't need to, and crash, we blame you. If you race above the speed limit, and lose control and crash, we blame you. If you—

CHARLES: Okay, so the moral is that if a driver takes all reasonable precautions, *then* he or she is off the hook. So suppose that as a matter of course "people seeds" drift through the air. Should such a seed find its way into your house, it can take root; and soon thereafter a developing fetus will be in place. I know this would be a weird world, but indulge me: imagine it with me for a minute. Now, suppose that you take precautions in light of the chance that seeds may root in your house. Suppose, for example, that you put up screens designed to keep people seeds from floating in.[5] Despite your precautions, however, a seed takes root, and consequently a fetus is in place. Would you now be obligated to nurture this fetus for nine months?

LAUREN: No. But you presume an analogy between putting up screens in the people-seed world and using birth control while having sex in this, the real one—and that, Charles, is yet *another* defective analogy. It's defective because people *choose* to have sex; people don't choose to exist and have a domicile in the people-seed world. (Presumably even in that world one exists because of amorous actions taken by others, and shelter is a sine qua non for staying alive.) To make the cases analogous, you would need to assume that in the seed world seeds would bombard a house if and only if its occupants performed some specific, avoidable action. But in that case, whether or not they put up the screens, I

---

5. This thought-experiment is due to Thomson ("A Defense of Abortion," *Philosophy and Public Affairs* (1971) **1.1**: 47–66), who (essentially) argues via it that if birth-control measures are taken, the parents are "off the hook."

would say that the owners of a house *are* responsible for a rooted seed, and therefore ought to nurture it.

Charles reflects.

LAUREN: Look, go back to the automotive case. Sometimes a motorist is blamed for injuries caused by an accident *even if* precautions are taken before setting out. When? It's simple: when the driver causes the accident. Having sex isn't like driving; having sex is like driving *and* racing through that yellow light. If a collision occurs, you're responsible. Likewise, if pregnancy ensues, those having sex are responsible.

Charles' expression reveals that he is still unconvinced.

CHARLES: No, in the case of driv—

ALEX: Excuse me for interrupting, but it seems to me that there is a quick way to ensure that the right sort of cases are being considered. We have only to return to the coma case that is at the heart of the antiabortion argument Charles is attacking and adapt this case so that it now accommodates the issues you two have been discussing.

Lauren and Charles both nod, reach for their mugs, and settle back a bit.

ALEX: Okay. You both remember the case, right? Amy has been thrown into a coma as a result of a car accident, so she doesn't have an inner life: she doesn't hope, reason, fear, judge, love, dream, plan, and so on. You are Amy's guardian; you have been informed that though she is currently in very tough shape, the prognosis is good: her score on the . . .

LAUREN: Glasgow Coma Scale.

ALEX: Right, thanks, is high enough for her to be considered "fully retrievable." Now, to adapt the case to fit your recent exchange, we may suppose that you have suddenly become Amy's guardian. And, following Lauren's point, we are forced to inject a feature that prevents a disanalogy: we are forced to assume that Amy and her misfortune have arisen and have come under your control, because of some actions you chose to perform—and you performed them knowing full well that Amy and her future might land in your lap.(Maybe you tried to fly through that yellow light.)

Now where do the two of you stand on the question of whether it's ethically permissible to pull the plug on Amy?

LAUREN: I think it would be downright evil to destroy her.

ALEX: Charles?

CHARLES: I am afraid I do not share Lauren's intuitions. They are certainly respectable intuitions, and they are consistent with her Hippocratic Oath, but I do not share them. If the odds of Amy's plight were low due to precautions you took, and if the trip that allowed Amy's plight to materialize was taken to secure highly desirable ends, then I'm just not sure. But I'm also not sure it matters—because I have stronger objections in mind.

Charles looks down to his notes.

LAUREN: Fire away.

CHARLES: Very well. Let me pull a page out of your own book, Lauren. You keep trying to trip me up on disanalogies in cases I claim are analogous to those arising in pregnancy. But is it really true that your own cornerstone case, as refined by Alex, that is the case involving Amy, is analogous to that which a mother faces in pregnancy? I don't think so; here's why.

The heart of the argument that so impresses you is really this claim. Because the fetus is an individual thing that *will become* a person with capacities allowing it to feel, reason, plan, love, hope, communicate, and so on—because the fetus, all things being equal, can have such a future—destroying it is tantamount to murder. Unfortunately, this claim is simply false. The problem is that in order for a thing to have a right to life, it must not only have a future in which it enjoys personhood, but it must also *have had,* over some interval of time in the past, the capacities from our list *L.*

Charles hunts for and finds the list on Lauren's placemat. He stabs it with the tip of his pen.

CHARLES: Now consider again your hypothetical accident victim, Amy, comatose but curable. I can pretty much agree with you that because Amy (given that she receives the necessary medical treatment) *will* once again have the capacity to feel, reason, plan, etc., destroying her is tantamount to murder. *But*—Amy had enjoyed these capacities in the past; the fetus has not. Ergo the two cases are disanalogous.[6]

Lauren pauses. She purses her lips, raises her eyebrows, and takes another sip.

ALEX: Are you sure that you understand the implications of your position, Charles? If you're right, it would seem to follow that infanticide is morally permissible. But infanticide, most would say, *isn't* morally permissible. Ergo, the objection fails.[7] And the reason why the objection countenances infanticide is—

LAUREN: —plain enough: the newborn infant hasn't in the past possessed capacities for reasoning and planning and desiring and so on. It's also plain enough that the antiabortion argument we're considering can be run in parallel so as to demonstrate that infanticide is morally wrong.[8] I take this to be evidence that my reasoning is sound.

Charles ponders. Then:

CHARLES: I concede that most of those in the pro-choice camp will find infanticide unpalatable. Faced with what the two of you have just said, such thinkers will doubtless hold that newborns *do* possess a capacity for reasoning and planning. For evidence, they might turn to what you, Lauren, are no doubt familiar with: the

6. This objection is a barbarically synoptic adaptation of part of the gist of Michael Tooley's seminal "A Defense of Abortion and Infanticide" from J. Feinberg, ed., *The Problem of Abortion* (Belmont, Cal.: Wadsworth), pp. 51–91.

7. Alex decides that it would be pedantic to inform the other two that the counterargument he just articulated conforms to the rule of inference known in logic as modus tollens, the general form of which is that from 'if p then q' and 'it's not the case that q' it follows that 'it's not the case that p.'

8. In a nutshell, the argument would run as follows. Infanticide is wrong because to kill an infant is to deprive it of a time when it will enjoy the fruits of personhood. More precisely, killing an infant is wrong because it is generally possible to ensure a certain chain of events that results in an infant enjoying the properties in the list L, and as such, by the Golden Principle, infants cannot be destroyed. What chain of events? The chain of events that most parents take it upon themselves to ensure with help from others, namely, the gradual nurturing of an infant into a toddler and beyond.

ability of newborns to recognize faces and to communicate with mother using prelinguistic sounds and body language.

LAUREN: Well, now wait a minute. I think I have to pull rank on this one. Sure, infants process information in remarkable ways—in ways medical science doesn't yet fully understand. But there is nothing like the powers enumerated in list £ in the picture!

CHARLES: No matter. The direction I'm personally inclined to take—and I know many on my side of the fence will find it misguided, at least at first—is to accept infanticide. Or at least I would say that infanticide is not *obviously* morally wrong. So to simply *assume* that it is is to beg the question against me. And *is* it really so easy to establish that infanticide is morally wrong—without simply recapitulating the line of argument you find persuasive in the case of abortion?

Lauren takes a deep breath and half frowns, half smiles. She is either unwilling or unable to competently embark upon an attempt to establish the immorality of infanticide.[9] Charles smiles broadly but without rancor and takes a sip of his coffee.

CHARLES: Lest you cling to your belief that infanticide is somehow self-evidently wrong, I give you the following case, which we might as well label the "Frankenstein case." Suppose that a scientist in the future, when the fields of artificial intelligence and biomechanical engineering have progressed, is able to build an artificial person.[10] Suppose, also, that everything is in place to

9. Readers wanting to pursue the issue are urged to begin with Tooley's classic paper. Tooley argues that if infanticide is wrong, then in a world in which cat brains can be injected with a chemical that turns them into human brains making suitable substrates for the capacities at the heart of personhood, it is obligatory that all cats be so injected. (The Frankenstein case that follows is also due to Tooley.) Evaluating this line of (imaginative!) reasoning will require considering analogies and disanalogies between "cat to person" development and fetus-to-person development. For useful remarks on the logical structure of analogical arguments, see my *What Robots Can and Can't Be*.

10. Here is a quote from Charniak and McDermott's *Introduction to Artificial Intelligence:* "The ultimate goal of AI research (which we are very far from achieving) is to build a person, or more humbly, an animal" (p. 7).

bring this person—let's call him Frank—to life. Would you say that before bringing Frank to life, the scientist is *obligated* to do so? If not, then how is it that the infant, *before he or she acquires the capacities at the heart of personhood,* must be preserved?

LAUREN: There is no *naturally occurring* causal chain that will bring the person Frank into existence. The situation is different with an infant: if nature is allowed to take it's course, the infant will soon develop into a person, a being having the properties on our list *L.*

CHARLES: But why should that be a morally relevant difference between the two cases? Suppose we change the Frankenstein scenario so that there is a naturally occ—

ALEX: Charles, if I may. Since the two of you seem to have reached a stalemate on this point, perhaps you should move on to your third objection.

An awkward silence. Lauren and Charles both look quizzically at Alex.

CHARLES: Stalemate? What stalemate? Such a declaration is as much in need of argument as the positions Lauren and I advocate.

Charles looks at Lauren, who nods agreement.

ALEX: Well, . . .

Alex struggles to gather his thoughts. This is the first time he has been knocked off balance. On what basis did he declare a stalemate if he is now extemporaneously assembling the rationale for the declaration?

ALEX: Okay. Let's take Charles' suggestion that the pre-person being in the Frankenstein case becomes a person by some naturally occurring process. Specifically, let's appeal to the idea of people seeds, which we briefly discussed a bit earlier: suppose that we can bring persons into existence by obtaining, planting, and nurturing people seeds. So let's imagine that Brown gets such a seed and plants it, and a process that will ultimately lead to the arrival of a person named Frank begins. If Brown decides to destroy the "embryo" after it reaches the halfway point in this process, what are we to say? I assume that Lauren would say that such an action by Brown may well be morally wrong. Lauren?

LAUREN: That's right. I wouldn't claim that Brown is definitely in the wrong here; I claim only that the moral status of Brown's "abortion" is unclear. And that fact should be enough to show that the Frankenstein case is ultimately unhelpful. In short, Charles, when your case is fleshed out to parallel the real-life process of pregnancy, it is no longer clear that it helps you.

CHARLES: Agreed. But since when is vagueness a virtue? You're missing the more fundamental problem that confronts you. Your argument's core concept, its very cornerstone, *personhood,* is intolerably vague. You say that personhood arises in some being when it enjoys the capacities enumerated in the list *L.* But how many of these capacities suffice to qualify a creature as a person? What do you do with those who only have *some* of these properties—the mentally retarded, say, who may not have the capacity to communicate in a language or the capacity to set plans and projects? And aren't a lot of the terms in *L* (for example, 'consciousness') painfully vague themselves?

LAUREN: I readily concede that 'person' is far from transparent; I can't define it precisely. In particular, even armed with the list *L* there will be recalcitrant cases. I concede, for example, that it *is* hard to ascertain whether a very severely retarded human being is a person. However, it is simply a non sequitur to conclude from the fact that a certain concept is vague that it is unsuitable for use in careful and productive reasoning. As Alex reminded us at the outset, many of the concepts in mathematics, that supposed bastion of precise and rigorous reasoning, cannot be defined.

Charles looks at Alex; Lauren follows suit.

ALEX: Well, it's certainly true that coming up with a precise definition of things like 'set' and 'number' has been well nigh impossible. Mathematicians—most, anyway—take such terms to be primitives. This practice goes all the way back to Euclid, who took as unanalyzed primitives such terms as 'point' and 'space'.

CHARLES: Some concepts are vague, and some are *vague.* I don't know that it's fair to lump 'number' and 'consciousness' together.

LAUREN: Why not? Neither can be defined, yet we use them constantly, and we know darn well what we mean when we deploy them.

And what about the legal realm, your own domain, Charles? Isn't it rife with concepts that admit of no precise definition? Consider 'reasonable doubt' and 'legally insane'—vague, yes, but sufficiently clear to base life-or-death decisions on. How much *less* vague, I would ask, is consciousness? We all know we're conscious; we all know what it's *like* to be conscious; we all know that to be conscious is rather important. Why should it matter for our purposes, then, if we can't *define* this phenomenon?

CHARLES: This is all too abstract. In *theory* the obscurity of personhood is not a problem. But let's bring things back to earth. What does your antiabortion stance dictate when the fetus has mild to moderate birth defects? Is abortion permissible or not?

LAUREN: Well, . . .

ALEX: I must insist on a point of logic, Charles—that is, if Lauren will allow me to interject.

Lauren gestures with an open palm for Alex to proceed.

ALEX: From the mere fact that it is difficult to determine whether some concept applies in some situation, it doesn't follow that that concept cannot generally do the job it is assigned to do. It is difficult, after all, to determine whether the concept of 'legally insane' applies in some situations, but it hardly follows that that this concept cannot generally accomplish the work it is assigned to do. Moreover, simply because some defendants may be neither clearly insane nor clearly sane doesn't entail that in a preponderance of cases it isn't clear which category applies and why it does.[11]

CHARLES: Fine. But I still don't have an answer. Again, what does your antiabortion stance dictate, Lauren, when the fetus has mild to moderate birth defects? Consider, *really* consider, the case of a retarded human being whose personhood is therefore in some doubt, or that of the fetus whose defects (disclosed, perhaps, from amniocentesis) make it unclear as to whether it will in the future enjoy the constellation of psychological capacities from L suffi-

11. Alex stops short of mentioning that the insanity defense has its roots in a notion quite relevant to our trio's investigation: viz., that a being who lacks some of the key capacities in list L is only a mere animal, not a person, and it makes little sense to punish or incarcerate a mere animal for a "crime."

cient to qualify it as a person. In these situations, how should we behave?

LAUREN: I confess that I don't know. But my ignorance shouldn't matter, for consider the following "hypo," to use your lingo. Suppose that Black goes into a park at night and begins shooting a machine gun into the darkness, at random. Such behavior, I hope we can agree, is immoral (all things being equal). Why is that? The answer should be obvious. Black's firing is immoral because he just might kill an innocent bystander.[12] Abortion, in cases where there is some question as to whether the fetus will develop into a person, is analogous to Black's behavior. Clearly, Black fails to provide an excuse for his lunacy if he says, "How can you be sure that my bullets will hit people? It's dark out here in the park." Just as clearly, the following doesn't seem to cut it: "How can you be sure that this abortion, on this fetus, will prevent a future person from existing? Perhaps the defects plaguing this fetus will prevent a sufficient number of the capacities in question from developing."

CHARLES: I don't buy it, Lauren. You're conveniently leaving out some key details. Suppose that Black is firing his gun not in a park, but in the deep woods, during hunting season. Why is it all right for Black to fire here?

LAUREN: You mean on the assumption that he has taken all the required precautions?

CHARLES: Exactly.

LAUREN: Well, if Black has abided by all the standard regulations and recommendations, when he fires, he won't kill another human. *That's* why it's all right for Black to fire.

CHARLES: But think a minute. Even in the deepest woods, isn't there still a chance that Black's firing will kill an innocent bystander? Maybe someone is out strolling in the woods, someone who didn't see the signs about hunting season being on. Maybe

12. The case just given, and the reasoning based upon it, are similar to ideas raised by J. T. Noonan in his "An Almost Absolute Value in History," in J. Feinberg, ed., *The Problem of Abortion* (Belmont, Cal.: Wadsworth, 1973), pp. 10–7.

another hunter is in Black's line of fire. Maybe Black has inadvertently ventured into terrain where people live, and a small cabin, unbeknownst to him, is in his line of fire. There are countless ways Black could kill another human by firing—and yet firing is permissible. How can that be?

Lauren's demeanor suggests that she has seen the point. She takes a sip of her coffee before responding.

LAUREN: The odds of Black's harming another human in the hunting scenario are *much* lower than in the park case.

CHARLES: That's right. And that implies that it's crucial to pin down the probabilities in the case of abortion when the fetus has a birth defect. But do you have the numbers handy? If the fetus has Down's Syndrome, is the probability .76 that it will be a person down the road? Or is it .45? Or maybe it's .675438?

LAUREN: What? Why do we have to know the actual probabilities? There is a nonvanishing probability that shifting in my seat while flying on a 747 will cause one of its doors to come loose and plummet to the ground, killing someone there.[13] If I can't calculate the probability in question, does that mean I must ride motionless in my seat, refuse coffee from the flight attendant? Hardly. Likewise, shooting in the hunting case is perfectly permissible.

CHARLES: Forgive me, Lauren, but you have a nose for the easy cases. What about the *hard* ones? I gave it already: what about a fetus with Down's Syndrome? What then?

LAUREN: *That's* a hard case? Many children with Down's Syndrome enjoy at least the bulk of the capacities from *L*. I know: I've cared for many of them in my practice. And, again, in any defect where there is an appreciable chance that the fetus will reach these capacities, common sense says to err on the side of caution.

Besides, you're back to your old dilemma. Since the vast majority of abortions are performed on fetuses having no serious defects, your objection does no damage to the view that abortion is, in the overwhelming majority of cases, immoral.

---

13. The probability of such an occurrence may be infinitesimal, but it is, as Lauren says, "nonvanishing." See N. Henderson, "New Door Latches Urged for Boeing 747 Jumbo Jets," *Washington Post*, 8/24/89.

CHARLES: But maybe your inability to firmly advise in the case of the troubled fetus indicates a more fundamental problem: maybe the concept of personhood at the heart of the antiabortion argument you affirm is *ridiculously* vague. After all, it would seem that if this argument is sound, artificial birth control is morally wrong, because the Golden Principle within it appears to apply to the gamete just as well as it applies to the fetus! But since—as I assume you agree—there's nothing wrong with artificial birth control, there's something very wrong with the argument.

Lauren pulls the list L in front of her and does the same with the antiabortion argument that deploys it; she reviews both. Then she takes a sip, reflects, and takes another sip. Presently:

LAUREN: No, you're wrong, Charles. The Golden Principle, in nutshell form, says that people in position to ensure that determinate individuals with the potential to enjoy the blessings of self-conscious, autonomous existence ought to ensure that that potential is realized. Artificial birth control doesn't contravene the Golden Principle in the least—for the simple reason that birth control is designed to prevent the existence of determinate individuals with the potentiality in question. There is no causal chain that takes the male gamete to personhood; neither is there a causal chain that takes the female gamete to personhood. Therefore the Golden Principle says nothing about how such entities are to be treated. It follows that the Golden Principle, contrary to your claim, does not prohibit artificial birth control. Once the two are fused, of course, the Golden Principle is in force.

CHARLES: Hmm. What you say implies that we aren't here.

LAUREN (*squinting*): What?

CHARLES: Well, think about it. You said that there is no causal chain running from the male or female gamete to personhood. But such a sequence of events is basically what brought the three of us into existence, no?

LAUREN: Maybe I'm just too subtle for you now and then, Charles. What I meant is that neither the male nor female gamete is a potential person. They are potential *parts* of a future person, yes, but so are all the molecules coming into a fetus's body for nourishment. The situation is radically different with the conceptus: it is a determinate object, and a very special one—one that has the potential to develop into a person. As such, the conceptus is covered by the Golden Principle.

CHARLES: I think you may well be splitting hairs, but at any rate, some birth control techniques work by destroying the conceptus, right? And as you have just asserted, the conceptus is covered by the Golden Principle—except in the exceptional cases we've uncovered.

LAUREN: Correct. For this reason the Golden Principle is consonant with papal prohibitions against "birth control" techniques in which the conceptus is destroyed. But these are not, strictly speaking, birth control techniques: they are abortions. Very *early* abortions are abortions nonetheless.

CHARLES: Okay, look. I'll grant, for the sake of argument, that the argument's prohibition against destroying the conceptus isn't counterintuitive—despite the fact that this prohibition will extend to birth control techniques most consider above reproach. But here's the second problem. Go back to the male and female gametes. Suppose that, as happens frequently, the use of a condom by a certain couple prevents fertilization of a certain egg. Would you agree that this behavior is morally permissible?

LAUREN: Yes.

CHARLES: Well, then you have a problem, because this behavior appears to be condemned by the reasoning you have embraced. Here's why. In this case, the egg is left unfertilized. Now, if the Golden Principle is to apply to this egg, these things must be true of it.

Charles circles the antecedent of the Golden Principle for Lauren, pencils in labels of 1 and 2 beside these points, and slides the relevant placemat over in front of her. What he has circled are the following two points:

- *x* is innocent, and

- *x* has, or *will* have—by virtue of a causal chain of events that can be kicked off by the actions of a person *y*—the capacities enumerated in list *L* (which together constitute personhood),

CHARLES: The egg qualifies. Clearly it's innocent if the conceptus is. Right?

LAUREN: Of course. But Charles, you're not reading the second point carefully enough.

Lauren taps the second clause.

LAUREN: It's just not true that the egg in question has or will have the capacities in *L*. I agree, of course, that *if* the condom hadn't been used, then by hypothesis the egg *would have* developed the capacities in question. But this fact doesn't cause the Golden Principle to kick in.

Charles wears an expression of genuine puzzlement.

ALEX: Excuse me for interrupting, Lauren, but I think you have gone wrong. You are certainly correct that the unfertilized female gamete in the condom case will never develop the capacities at the core of personhood. But that can't be what exempts this entity from coverage by the Golden Principle. After all, suppose someone kills a fetus and then serenely says to you, "I've done nothing wrong, Lauren, not even according to your own code. Because this fetus here is now dead, and a dead anything will not develop the capacities on your list *L*."

The reason why this is sophistry (by your own antiabortion lights) is that there was a point in time when it was true to say that the fetus will, ceteris paribus, become a bearer of the capacities that constitute personhood.

CHARLES: But then I can say the same thing about the unfertilized egg in the condom case. There was a point in time, namely that time before the condom was used, when it was true to say that the egg in question would develop into a being having the capacity for self-consciousness, communication, and so on for the rest of *L*.

ALEX: Lauren?

Lauren thinks, her cheeks clasped in her hands, her elbows on the table . . .

LAUREN: Now wait a minute. It just isn't true that the egg in the condom case will develop into a person. It's the *fertilized* egg that will develop this way. And that's why it's the fertilized egg, the conceptus, that cannot be destroyed. There's a genuine and important difference here, one that explains why using a condom (and other similar techniques) is perfectly permissible.

CHARLES: No, sorry, you still have a problem on your hands when it comes to birth control. To say that the conceptus will develop into a being having the capacities enumerated in *L* is to admit that, if not meddled with, it will grow and change; it will take on things from outside it for energy and expend that energy in its development. Why isn't the same thing true of the unfertilized egg? Isn't it true that if it isn't meddled with, it too will take elements from outside it—the sperm, for example—and proceed to develop into a person?

Lauren reflects yet again. Her energy level, as well as Charles's, is as high as ever.

LAUREN: But there's a difference. The concep—

ALEX: I'm sorry, but I'm inclined to call your clash a tie at this point. Perhaps the two of you will agree that I've delivered on my promise. We have on the table what would appear to be the most powerful antiabortion argument we can muster—but, promising as it is, it isn't compelling, as Charles' objections have demonstrated. Now I know that the two of you will disagree with my judgment. Lauren, you think that the argument in question is sound. Charles, you think it *isn't* sound. But I submit that a third-party observer would have to think hard before rendering his or her own verdict. So I suggest—

CHARLES: Again!

Charles looks at Lauren.

CHARLES: He's doing it again, no?

Lauren signals agreement with a nod.

LAUREN: You *are* doing it again.

ALEX: What?

LAUREN: You're calling a tie with plenty of time left on the clock, and plenty of energy left in the players. And you know what, Alex? I think at this point that maybe Charles and I are growing a bit . . . well, a bit *skeptical*.

Alex stares at Lauren. There is silence as she returns his gaze.

ALEX: I don't follow.

LAUREN: Well, what sort of agnostic are you? At the very start of our discussions, you said that you were agnostic about God's existence. I took that to mean that you don't believe God exists, and you don't believe God *doesn't* exist.

ALEX: Right, that's me.

LAUREN: But what do you believe about your attitude? Do you believe it must be permanent? Do you believe that nothing could come to your attention that might dissolve your agnosticism in favor of a stand one way or the other?

ALEX: Of course not. As an agnostic I'm always on the prowl for new evidence that could settle the question.

CHARLES: That's what I thought. But then why don't you let Lauren and me settle the issue? She believes abortion is almost always immoral; I think it's almost always permissible. But I think we both believe that one of us is right, that one of us is wrong, *and* that we can discover which is which.

Charles looks at Lauren, who nods to say Absolutely.

CHARLES: And look, Alex, at the progress you've catalyzed! We have agreed that the mere humanity of the fertilized egg doesn't give it moral standing. We have agreed that abortion is permissible in cases where a fetus will not develop sufficiently to become a person. We have agreed that on the table before us is a formidable antiabortion argument—which Lauren has so far ably defended, but which I have not finished attacking. We have even agreed on a number of exceptions to this argument.

Lauren writes out these exceptions now, and slides the result—

1 severe birth defects;

2. parents unable to secure properties from *L* for the fetus;

3. rape;
4. e.g., ectopic pregnancy $\left.\right\}$ self-defense

—in front of Alex. He glances down, assimilates them quickly.

Alex: All right, sorry. We *have* established a lot, and I know the two of you are ready to make even more progress—but could I ask you to spend some time considering the future with me? My question, specifically, is this: Given what we have discovered so far, what would it take for Supreme Court justices to overturn, in reasoned fashion, *Roe* v. *Wade?* I assume that both of you are acutely interested in this question—but for radically different reasons.

Charles and Lauren look at each other.

Lauren: It's a good question.

Charles: Indeed. But perhaps some dessert first?

The other two agree without hesitation. Charles rises and makes his way toward the counter, wherein rests his favorite since his first year at Georgetown Law: tiramisu.

Chapter 6

Abortion, the Law, and the Future

The three are settled back at their table, coffee and dessert sitting upon it. Alex finishes his tiramisu and leaves his spoon in the empty parfait goblet with a clink.

ALEX: So, the question now before us is: What might it take for federal law on abortion to be overturned on the basis of argument? Perhaps we should start by evaluating the reasoning behind *Roe* v. *Wade*. Here again I think slavery can prove illuminating. Are the two of you at least somewhat familiar with the Court's original ruling on slavery?

CHARLES: Dred Scott?

ALEX: Exactly. Can you give us the facts of the case?

CHARLES: Sure. I know them through and through, learned them all for Law School.
  Dred Scott, born at the turn of the century, was owned during his first thirty years by the Blow family. When Peter Blow died in 1832, Scott was sold for five hundred dollars to an army surgeon, Dr. John Emerson of St. Louis, whose career took him and Scott to Missouri, Illinois, and what is now Minnesota. When Emerson died, his wife received title to Dred, and the slave tried to purchase his freedom from Mrs. Emerson. When this attempt failed, he sued for his freedom in St. Louis circuit court in April of . . . let's see . . . 1846.

The Opinion of the Supreme Court regarding Dred Scott's claim was written by Chief Justice Taney,[1] who held that Scott did not qualify as a person under the Constitution, nor under the Declaration of Independence. Taney reasoned that slaves, at the time the Constitution was drafted, were considered an inferior class of being, who had been subjugated by the dominant race and, whether emancipated or not, yet remained subject to their authority and had no rights or privileges of their own.

As Taney put it, blacks

> had for more than a century before been regarded as beings of an inferior order, and altogether unfit to associate with the white race, either in social or political relations; and so far inferior, that they had no rights which the white man was bound to respect; and the negro might justly and lawfully be reduced to slavery for his benefit (p. 13).

ALEX: Thank you, Charles. Now correct me if I'm wrong, but as I recall, Taney's argument can be paraphrased as follows.

The Constitution and Declaration of Independence ascribe unalienable rights to a class of beings known as persons. It is undeniable, then, that *if* the slave is covered by these key terms from these documents, slavery ought immediately to be declared immoral and illegal. But these terms *do not* apply to slaves, as is easily seen by the following reasoning. If slaves *were* covered under this language, then the conduct of the men who framed the great documents in question (since they themselves owned slaves) would have been inconsistent with the documents. But these were indeed great men—men incapable of such inconsistency. Therefore the language in question excludes the negro slave.

CHARLES: That's Taney's argument exactly. As he put it, if the language in question embraced the African race,

> the conduct of the distinguished men who framed the Declaration of Independence would have been utterly and flagrantly

---

1. Not all agreed with all aspects of Taney's ruling. In fact, every member of the Court filed comment, and Curtis wrote in vehement dissent.

inconsistent with the principles they asserted . . . yet the men who framed this declaration were great men—high in literary acquirements—high in their sense of honor, and incapable of asserting principles inconsistent with those on which they were acting (p. 14).

ALEX: So Taney here committed, in a way that sustains his words in perpetual infamy, the *fallacy of appeal to authority,* wherein one infers from the mere fact that some authority is an authority that it isn't mistaken. Today, we realize that the framers, however illustrious in other matters, *were* inconsistent in this sphere.[2]

CHARLES: Maybe it's just the lawyer in me, but it seems odd to criticize the Court for appealing to authority when the practice of citing precedent is a central tradition in legal argument; maybe we can take this up later. Right now I want to know what all this has to do with *Roe* v. *Wade.* Are you claiming that Taney's argument parallels that given in the majority opinion in *Roe* v. *Wade?*

ALEX: Maybe, maybe not. Just as I'm agnostic on the abortion controversy from the perspective of morality, so I'm agnostic on the question of whether the main argument in *Roe* v. *Wade* is sound. But I do believe that the reasoning in *Roe* v. *Wade* is at least suspicious, logically speaking, and that this fact, combined with the antiabortion argument we've explored today, the argument Lauren embraces and you, Charles, still reject, can point the way toward a future in which *Roe* v. *Wade* is overturned. This would be a future Lauren, despite her willingness to accept a list of permissible abortions, would presumably welcome and a future you, Charles, would want to anticipate and prevent.

But before we go any further, we need a brief review of the facts in *Roe* v. *Wade.* I bet Lauren can help us here.

LAUREN: Indeed I can.[3]

2. Some of them, e.g., Thomas Jefferson, *knew* they were inconsistent. For a wonderful discussion of this issue, see Ronald Dworkin's *Life's Dominion.*

3. Lauren used to say that the facts in question were like a dagger in her heart, but such a phrase now strikes her as almost . . . stupidly unhelpful.

The skeletal facts of the 1972 case are as follows. A pregnant single woman (Roe) sought a judgment "on behalf of herself and all other women" that the Texas statutes declaring abortion a crime (save when performed to protect the life of the mother) violated her right to personal privacy, as secured in the First, Fourth, Fifth, Ninth, and Fourteenth Amendments of the Constitution. The opinion of the Court, delivered by Blackmun, and joined by Douglas, Brennan, Stewart, Marshall, and Powell, gave Roe victory. Douglas and Stewart filed concurring opinions; White filed a dissenting opinion in which Rehnquist joined.

Lauren looks at Charles, who indicates that she is on target.

ALEX: What sort of reasoning did the Court offer in support of its opinion?

LAUREN: The Court[4] conceded—and, in fact, so did appellee and appellant—that if the fetus were a person, the Fourteenth Amendment would guarantee it a right to life, and that right would override Roe's right to privacy.[5] But immediately after this concession the Court reasoned as follows:

'Person', though used repeatedly in the Constitution, is not defined therein. Moreover, when used in this document, and when used in 19th century abortion statutes (both in America and in English Common Law), it has application only postnatally. This—and, thanks to many a late-night study session, I quote—

---

4. I do not include discussion of the fact that the Court's opinion in *Roe v. Wade* seeks an answer to When does human life begin? in order to adjudicate Roe's claim. (For perhaps direct treatment of this issue, see V.3, p. 133.) As our three discussants have seen, this question is quite easily answered but also quite possibly irrelevant to the abortion controversy. By the principle of charity in such matters, I follow Chisholm ("Coming Into Being and Passing Away: Can the Metaphysician Help?" in S. F. Spicker and H. T. Engelhardt, Jr., eds., *Philosophical Medical Ethics: Its Nature and Significance* (Dordrecht, The Netherlands: D. Reidel, 1977), pp. 169–82) in interpreting the reasoning of the Court not as an attempt to grapple with this probable red herring but rather as an attempt to settle the perhaps more relevant question of when *personhood* begins.

5. There are many situations wherein the right to privacy is overridden, of course. Your right to privacy does not afford you the freedom to cultivate a cocaine plantation on your own acreage, for example.

"persuades us that the word 'person,' as used in the Fourteenth Amendment, does not refer to the unborn."[6]

ALEX: Now, do either of you see anything suspicious about this reasoning? If not, let me explain an elementary logical fallacy known as begging the question, or, in the Latin, *petitio principii*. To beg the question is to take as premise that which you seek to establish. For example, suppose that one party in a debate about whether America should provide financial aid to foreign countries offers this argument.

Alex writes out the following argument and shows it first to Lauren and then to Alex.

Fallacy$_1$

(1) Foreign aid is a bad idea.

∴ (2) Foreign aid is a bad idea.

ALEX: Is that a valid argument?

CHARLES: Of course not. That which is to be shown is taken as a premise.[7] And you're suggesting that the Court's reasoning in *Roe v. Wade* is similarly defective?

For reply, Alex writes out the following argument on one of the placemats, and passes it to the other two.

---

6. See Section IX, Opinion of the Court, pp. 156–58.

7. Here is a more subtle instance of the very same fallacy (which Alex scrawled out but decided not to discuss):

Fallacy$_2$

(3) Either God exists or $3 + 3 = 7$.

(4) It's not true that $3 + 3 = 7$.

∴ (5) God exists.

Obviously, no one skeptical about the first premise, (3), is going to accept the conclusion, (5). Premise (4) is of course true.

Fallacy$_3$

(6) The term 'person' as used in the Constitution does not apply to the unborn.

∴ (7) The term 'person' as used in the Constitution does not apply to the unborn.

LAUREN: The problem with this argument is that (6) is itself the issue. Everyone knows that the Constitution doesn't say, "Oh, hey, by the way, the term 'person' used herein applies to the fetus." The challenge is to figure out, by using one's brain, if this term, as used in the Constitution, *ought* to be construed as applying to the unborn. Likewise, in the sad case of *Scott* v. *Sanford*, it was well known that the Constitution didn't at the time declare, "Oh, hey, by the way, the term 'person' used herein applies to slaves." The principal task facing the Taney Court was to ascertain whether or not the term 'person' (and 'citizen') *ought* to be construed as applying to slaves—a task that, as we have seen, the Court failed miserably to meet.

CHARLES: Wait a minute. Justices are charged with determining the original *intent* of the legislators who make law, as well as, by examination of precedent, the reading of that law in prior judicial rulings. In *Roe* v. *Wade* the question is whether the constitution treats fetuses as persons. The justices peruse it, along with other laws, and decide it does not. Where is the fallacy?

LAUREN: Charles, just because the reasoning in question is used all the time by your colleagues doesn't mean that the reasoning isn't fallacious. To infer from the fact that jurists routinely reason in accordance with some pattern that that pattern isn't fallacious is itself a fallacy!

Lauren's syntax brings a smile to each face.

LAUREN: Seriously, you know what? Rendering judgments on the basis of prior intent and precedent, for profound constitutional issues, may well be "intrinsically" fallacious. Judgments rendered on the basis of precedent necessarily involve an inference to some proposition based merely on the fact that that proposition has in the past been affirmed—and this inference, as Alex points out, has been classified for centuries, justifiably, as a fallacy.

CHARLES: But argument from precedent and original intent, which I grant is one of the fundamental modes of reasoning in common law jurisprudence (as opposed to the civil law scheme that prevails outside England and the United States), can be valid if at the starting point in the chain of appeal to prior cases someone has got things right.

LAUREN: Agreed. But has a majority of our Supreme Court justices at some previous point gotten things right when it comes to matters crucially connected to personhood? Certainly they didn't have things straight when it came to dealing with slavery.

CHARLES: But the Court rectified the situation. It agreed, later, that slaves were persons, and that as such they must be accorded liberty.[8] Abortion is different. It's self-evident that blacks are persons: they possess all the attributes enumerated in our list *L*. As we've seen, things are rather more controversial when it comes to the fetus!

LAUREN: Again, agreed. But the point—one which you seem to be doing your best to dodge—is this: It doesn't follow from the fact that precedent classifies the fetus as a nonperson that the fetus *is* a nonperson.

CHARLES: I gladly concede the point. But you must likewise concede that some additional argument must be provided to the effect that the fetus is a person. Even if *Roe* v. *Wade* is fallacious, we are left with the absence of this additional argument. Now I know you think we uncovered this argument earlier, but the fact is, I still do not accept it. Let me get back to *why* I do not. You see—

ALEX: Before the two of you resume, let me give you a possible *second* fallacy to chew on: the fallacy of appeal to authority, the very same fallacy that, as we have seen, was flagrantly committed in Taney's spurious reasoning. The inference in question is this one.

Alex turns again to the placement:

8. Charles decides to steer clear of the view, shared by many of his colleagues, that the Court's rulings are definitive. As Charles knows, Dred Scott was overturned by a constitutional amendment, not by a determination that the Court erred.

Fallacy$_4$

(8) Jurists in England and America hold a position which entails that the 14th Amendment doesn't apply to the fetus.

∴ (9) The 14th Amendment doesn't apply to the fetus.

He slides what he has written in front of the pediatrician.

ALEX: Lauren?

LAUREN: Even if we concede premise (8), the conclusion, (9), does not follow. If it *did* follow, slavery would be morally permissible, because, as we already saw, the very same reasoning not only can be but *was* given in defense of slavery by Chief Justice Taney and his colleagues. Since slavery is *not* morally permissible, we can safely conclude that Blackmun's reasoning is invalid.

Lauren picks up her coffee cup, takes a sip, returns it to the table, and throws a friendly but challenging look at Charles.

CHARLES: But contrary to what you suggest, Lauren, the Court dealt only with a *legal* issue, not a moral one. Still, it doesn't matter, for I happily concede that some of the reasoning in *Roe v. Wade* is—what was Alex's word?—suspicious. What you fail to realize is that all this reasoning can be rather quickly repaired. Here, I'll even employ a key aspect of our earlier debate: the list L.

Charles begins setting out a new argument. After a minute, he slides the following in front of Lauren.

Fix of Fallacy$_4$

(10) If something doesn't possess the properties constitutive of personhood, namely, the properties listed in L, then the 14th Amendment does not apply to that thing.

(11) The fetus does not possess the properties in L (as jurists in England and America, including those involved in *Roe v. Wade*, have observed).

∴ (12) The 14th Amendment does not apply to the fetus.

Lauren reads the argument.

LAUREN: Hmm . . .

She looks up at Charles.

ALEX: Dare I say it: a draw?

Lauren and Charles both look at Alex, both shake their heads, and both frown.

LAUREN: No, *don't* say it.

Then, to Charles, tapping his premise (11) with her pencil:

LAUREN: But the fetus *does* have the properties in *L*. Apparently you have never faced up to th—

ALEX: Okay, look, no draw. Fair enough. But before you two heat it up again, I press the question once more: How might it come about that the law on abortion changes on the strength of reason?

CHARLES: Well, the Court held that the unborn do not have a right to life under the Fourteenth Amendment. But the question, given our discussion here today, might be What about *potential* persons? The case against abortion assembled in our earlier dialectic, the case Lauren likes, hinges on the claim that potential persons have rights nearly on par with the persons they will, all things being equal, become.

LAUREN: So, if the Fourteenth Amendment were construed so as to afford protection to potential persons, abortion could be deemed illegal. And the argument supporting this construal could be one we three now know well: that since a right to life is granted certain comatose patients in virtue of the fact that they will once again enjoy those psychological capacities we treasure, the same must be granted to the unborn, who are more likely than the comatose to reach these capacities.

CHARLES: I'll be sure to stay vigilant, Lauren.

LAUREN: And well you should. For there is already, in the original decision, an opening, a door standing invitingly ajar. As we have seen, the Opinion of the Court in *Roe* v. *Wade* was based in no small part upon the rationale that the framers of the Constitution did not intend to have the rights of persons extend to the unborn. On the other hand, the Court was quite comfortable issuing a judgment they believed the framers would have issued had they known what we know now.[9] Well, one of the things we know now is that, in situations involving brain trauma that was unmanageable in the framers' era, we are obligated to intervene medically in order to respect the injured's right to life. Right?

CHARLES: Right.

LAUREN: Well, perhaps as our knowledge of the brain increases, and our ability to heal neurological damage increases in concert with this growing knowledge, there will arise a common and unwavering belief that having a future in which personhood blossoms is sufficient to secure the right to life.

Charles looks at her. Then, good naturedly:

CHARLES: Does this all boil down, then, to doctors versus lawyers?

Lauren smiles a full, unrestrained smile.

CHARLES: But you know what, Lauren? Fine. Say it happens. Let us suppose that this future you so desire, fueled by advances in medical technology, comes to pass. There is a problem you have yet to face: if—

ALEX: Sorry, you two, but I'm afraid we now sit here all alone, the coffee machines off and cleaned, the front door long locked, and Bert standing by the back door with the partisan things the two of you checked in upon entering.

Charles and Lauren look together toward Bert, who indeed stands as Alex has described him. The three rise (Alex quickly folds up and pockets the placemats for posterity) and head toward the exit. They thank Bert and shake his hand. Charles and Lauren take their placards from him (Lauren takes her mock casket as well; Charles takes his coat hanger) and exit. Once outside the three find themselves in a back alley, beside a dumpster.

___

9. As Rehnquist pointed out in his dissenting opinion, surely the drafters of the Fourteenth Amendment did not intend that pregnancy be divided (à la the Blackmun, Opinion-of-the-Court scheme) into three distinct trimesters, with different regulations governing each of the three intervals. Such a tripartite division, as Rehnquist says, "partakes of judicial legislation." The rebuttal to this charge is presumably that *if* the framers had known what we know now (about, e.g., fetal development, etc.), they would have affirmed the tripartite division.

ALEX: Bert probably wouldn't mind your borrowing his garbage service.

Charles and Lauren grasp the veiled suggestion, but both slip their placards back on.

LAUREN: Alex, you want to join us? Maybe I can win you over to my side.

CHARLES: Or *my* side.

Alex pauses. Then:

ALEX: Sure. Plato's?

CHARLES: Two blocks, right?

ALEX: Yup.

CHARLES: Good. With a leisurely pace, maybe, just maybe, I can settle this thing before we get there.

The three walk off slowly down the alley toward the main street.

CHARLES: All right, we come now to the protest that appears here.

Charles stops and slaps his placard: ABORTION SAVES LIVES!

CHARLES: As I was saying, Lauren, let us suppose for the sake of argument that the future you dream of does arrive. The problem is that the policies you would put in place are, to put it brutally, heartless and prejudicial. If abortion becomes illegal (save, of course, for the rare exceptions we have discussed), those ill equipped to bring children to term would be forced to do so. This would bring Draconian suffering and hardship to the weakest and poorest among us. The wealthy, on the other hand, with all the resources they have at their disposal, would find it relatively easy to manage.

LAUREN: You're attacking a straw woman! Today's core antiabortion argument is one purporting to show that abortion is almost always immoral; it is that and only that. The argument says nothing about public policy. Lord knows, I'm not a public policy pundit; I'm a doctor and a mother. It is the *government's* job to figure out how to apply the law in as fair and equitable a manner as possible.

CHARLES: That's a dodge.

LAUREN: On the contrary, it's a fact. And here's another relevant one. The law is *currently* applied inequitably with respect to economic status. No one in his or her right mind can deny this, least of all you; you see it up close and personal, I assume. If, in our legal system, two men, one a multimillionaire and one a pauper, are accused of murder in cases exactly similar except for the financial reserves involved, who will mount a first-rate defense? The rich man will have an army of relentless legal minds of the first rank; the poor man will have one young lawyer working for a veritable pittance. The result of such a chasm has been played out repeatedly in recent times. In light of this, if your current objection is cogent, it follows that we must revoke our laws against murder. I don't think that's a palatable consequence, do you?

Charles frowns to concede the point, begins walking down the alley again. The other two fall in beside him.

LAUREN: Besides, aren't there practical steps our society could take to soften the blow of new antiabortion statutes? For one thing, there could be a concerted effort to crack down on the men responsible for unwanted pregnancies. As things stand now, the women bear the bulk of the burden. That is horribly unfair. The men responsible for the plight of these women should be compelled by law to economically and emotionally support, to the fullest of their ability, the mother and child for many years. I suspect that if such a policy were implemented, even in the absence of the new antiabortion laws I desire, a marked decline in the number of abortions would result.

CHARLES: Fair enough. Such a policy marks yet another point of agreement between us. Of course, I still don't . . .

Bert steps out, bolts his rear door, turns, and pauses. He watches the silhouettes of his last three customers recede into the darkness and takes note of the fact that their voices are too low—too rational?—to make out.

Chapter 7

Placemats for Posterity

Alex saved the plaements; here they are . . .

A person
1. is conscious;
2. communicates through a language;
3. knows and believes things;
4. desires things;
5. is self-conscious;
6. has a "will"; and
7. reasons.

} L →

A person is a being having the capacity to
1. be conscious;
2. communicate through a language;
3. know and believe things;
4. desire things;
5. be self-conscious;
6. "will"; and
7. reason.

Ex of Fallacy:

(a) If something doesn't possess the properties constitutive of personhood namely the properties listed in L, then the 14th Amendment does not apply to that thing.

(b) The fetus does not possess the properties in L (or justifiably - in England and America, including those involved in Roe v. Wade, have observed)

∴ (c) The 14th Amendment does not apply to the fetus.

The Proof That Slavery Is Morally Wrong

Theorem: Slavery is morally wrong.

Proof: If X is an innocent person, then Killing (maiming, torturing, incarcerating, whipping, selling, etc.) X is morally wrong. John is an innocent person. Ergo, Striker's treatment of John is morally wrong. QED

The (explicit) Proof That Slavery Is Wrong

Theorem: Slavery is morally wrong.

Proof: If X is an innocent person then killing (maiming, torturing, incarcerating, whipping, selling, etc.) X is morally wrong — unless such treatment prevents an extra ordinary catastrophe that is itself a horrible evil. John is an innocent person. Striker's treatment of John does not prevent an extraordinary catastrophe that is itself a horrible evil. Ergo, Striker's treatment of John is morally wrong. Since 'Striker' and 'John' are names used to stand for any master and slave, respectively, what we have inferred about them can be inferred about slave owners and slaves in general; from which it follows that the institution of slavery is morally wrong. QED

- How can you tell when something is human?
- How can you tell when something is alive?

Definition of Life

1. Life a pattern, not a specific material object.
2. Self-reproduction.
3. Storage of self-representation.
4. Metabolism.
5. Interactions with the environment.
6. Interdependence of parts.
7. Stability.
8. Ability to evolve.

Fallacy,
(1) Foreign aid is a bad idea.
∴ (2) Foreign aid is a bad idea.

Fallacy₂
(3) Either God exists or 3+3=7.
(4) It's not true that 3+3=7.
∴ (5) God exists.

Fallacy₃
(6) The term 'person' as used in the Constitution does not apply to the unborn.
∴ (7) The term 'person' as used in the constitution does not apply to the unborn.

Fallacy₄
(8) Jurists in England and America hold a position which entails that the 14th Amendment doesn't apply to the fetus.
∴ (9) The 14th Amendment doesn't apply to the fetus.

The Case £1 Proof That Slavery Is Wrong

Theorem. Slavery is morally wrong.

Proof. If x is innocent, and has the capacities enumerated in L, then killing (maiming, torturing, incarcerating, whipping, selling, etc.) x is morally wrong—unless such treatment prevents an extraordinary catastrophe that is itself a horrible evil. John is innocent and (even while asleep) has the capacities listed in L. Striker's treatment of John (whipping, killing,... him) does not prevent an extraordinary catastrophe that is itself a horrible evil. Ergo, Striker's treatment of John is morally wrong. Since 'striker' and 'John' are names picked at random, what we have inferred about them can be inferred about slave owners and slaves in general, from which it follows that the institution of slavery is morally wrong. QED.

The Silver Principle

If
• x is innocent, and
• x has the capacities enumerated in lis L (which, taken together, say what it is to be a person), then killing (etc.) x is morally wrong — unless such treatment prevents an extraordinary catastrophe that is itself a horrible evil.

The Golden Principle

If
• x is innocent, and
• x has, or will have — because of a chain of events that can be kicked off by a person y — the capacities enumerated in list L (which together constitute personhood),

then it is morally wrong for y to destroy, or to authorize others to destroy, x — unless such destruction prevents an extraordinary catastrophe that is itself a horrible evil.

Problems :

The Anti-abortion Argument

Theorem. Abortion, except in certain exceedingly rare cases, is morally wrong.

Proof. First, we reiterate the Golden Principle:

If X
- is innocent, and
- has, or will have —by virtue of a causal chain of events that can be enabled by the actions of a person— the capacities enumerated in list L,

then it is morally wrong for y to destroy, or to authorize others to destroy, X — unless such destruction prevents an extraordinary catastrophe that is itself a horrible evil.

Next, consider some fetus F and some parent P. Fetuses are innocent (since they have done nothing to threaten others — a fetus can't really do anything, after all); hence F is innocent. P, since for some rare cases, has it within his or her power to enable a causal chain of events leading to a point in time when the fetus F will have the capacities at the heart of personhood enumerated in list L. (It follows immediately that it is morally wrong for P to destroy F, which if to say (since F and P are general variables, standing for any fetus and parent) abortion is morally wrong. QED

EXCEPTIONS: ① severe birth defects; ② parents unable to secure properties from L for fetus; ③ rape; ④ e.g., ectopic pregnancy

Self-defense

Bibliography

Bringsjord, S. (1992) *What Robots Can and Can't Be* (Dordrecht, The Netherlands: Kluwer).

Charniak, E., and McDermott, D. (1985) *Introduction to Artificial Intelligence* (Reading, Mass.: Addison-Wesley).

Chisholm, R. M. (1977) "Coming Into Being and Passing Away: Can the Metaphysician Help?" in S. F. Spicker and H. T. Engelhardt, Jr., eds., *Philosophical Medical Ethics: Its Nature and Significance* (Dordrecht, The Netherlands: D. Reidel), pp. 169–82.

Dennett, D. (1976) "Conditions of Personhood," in A. O. Rorty, ed., *The Identities of Persons* (Berkeley, Cal.: University of California Press), pp. 175–96.

Dworkin, R. (1994) *Life's Dominion* (New York: Random House).

Ebbinghaus, H. D., Flum, J., and Thomas, W. (1984) *Mathematical Logic* (New York: Springer-Verlag).

English, J. (1975) "Wrongs and Rights," *The Canadian Journal of Philosophy* **5.2:** 233–43.

Farmer, J. D., and Belin, A. (1992) "Artificial Life: The Coming Evolution," in C. G. Langton et al., *Artificial Life II* (Redwood City, Cal.: Addison-Wesley), pp. 815–40.

Feinberg, J., ed. (1973) *The Problem of Abortion* (Belmont, Cal.: Wadsworth).

Kunda, Z. (1990) "The Case for Motivated Reasoning," *Psychological Bulletin* **108:** 480–98.

Kutler, S. I., ed. (1967) *The Dred Scott Decision: Law or Politics?* (Boston, Mass.: Houghton Mifflin).

Langton, C. G., et al., eds. (1992) *Artificial Life II* (Redwood City, Cal.: Addison-Wesley).

Marquis, D. (1989) "Why Abortion Is Immoral," *Journal of Philosophy* **89:** 185–202.

Noonan, J. T. (1973) "An Almost Absolute Value in History," in J. Feinberg, ed., *The Problem of Abortion* (Belmont, Cal.: Wadsworth), pp. 10–7.

Russell, S. and Norvig, P. (1995) *Artificial Intelligence: A Modern Approach* (Englewood Cliffs, N.J.: Prentice-Hall).

Spafford, E. H. (1992) "Computer Viruses: A Form of Artificial Life?" in C. G. Langton et al., *Artificial Life II* (Redwood City, Cal.: Addison-Wesley), pp. 727–45.

Thomson, J. J. (1971) "A Defense of Abortion," *Philosophy and Public Affairs* **1.1:** 47–66.

Tooley, M. (1973) "A Defense of Abortion and Infanticide," in J. Feinberg, ed., *The Problem of Abortion* (Belmont, Cal.: Wadsworth), pp. 51–91.

Wright, R., Dibbell, J., and Kasparov, G. (1996) "Can Machines Think?" *Time* **147.13:** 50–8.

The author would welcome your comments about this dialogue:

Selmer Bringsjord
Associate Professor
Department of Philosophy, Psychology, and Cognitive Science
Rensselaer Polytechnic Institute
Troy, New York 12180
selmer@rpi.edu
http://www.rpi.edu/~brings

Introductory Dialogues from Hackett

Abortion:
A Dialogue
by Selmer Bringsjord

Mind and Brain:
A Dialogue on the Mind-Body Problem
by Rocco J. Gennaro

Can Animals and Machines Be Persons?
by Justin Leiber

Posthumous Meditations
by W. A. McMullen

Who's to Say?
A Dialogue on Relativism
by Norman Melchert

Does God Exist?
A Dialogue
by Todd C. Moody

A Dialogue on Personal Identity and Immortality
by John R. Perry

Mind, Man, and Machine
Second Edition
by Paul T. Sagal

Introducing the Existentialists:
Imaginary Interviews with Sartre, Heidegger, and Camus
by Robert Solomon

Introducing the German Idealists:
Mock Interviews with Kant, Hegel, and Others
by Robert Solomon

Invitation to Philosophy:
Imagined Dialogues with Great Philosophers
by Yuval Steinitz

Free Will and Determinism
by Clifford Williams

More Advanced Dialogues

Philosophy in Play:
Three Dialogues
by Ermanno Bencivenga

Freedom:
A Dialogue
by Ermanno Bencivenga